ENEMY
IN THE MIRROR

Winning the
Warfare of the Mind

Dr. Lonny Bingle

insight *publishing group*

Tulsa, Oklahoma

ENEMY IN THE MIRROR: WINNING THE WARFARE OF THE MIND

Enemy in the Mirror by Dr. Lonny Bingle
Published by Insight Publishing Group
8801 S. Yale, Suite 410
Tulsa, OK 74137
918-493-1718

ISBN 1-930027-50-8
Library of Congress catalog card number: 2002100102

Printed in the United States of America

Contents

Dedication
Acknowledgments
Endorsements
Foreword
Preface

Chapter One
The Arena of Spiritual Warfare
19

Chapter Two
Truth vs. Fact
29

Chapter Three
Ministering to the Heart
39

Chapter Four
Knowing God's Nature
47

Chapter Five
Who Am I?
55

Chapter Six
Walking Like Jesus
65

Chapter Seven
The Armor of God
75

Chapter Eight
Demonic Warfare
83

Chapter Nine
The Ultimate Enemy
95

Chapter Ten
Renewing the Mind
103

Chapter Eleven
Finally
113

Dedication

To my loving wife, Kim. You are the best thing that has ever happened in my life. Without you and your understanding, I do not believe I would be in ministry today. Your heart of compassion for people is a constant reminder of our calling together. I love you with all of my heart and thank God daily for your wisdom and help.

To our four children Joshua, Jonathan, Jason, and Krysta. Daddy loves you very much and I want you to know that I realize the sacrifices you make sharing me with so many people. You are such a vital part of my life and I am so thankful you are my children. Always remember to put God first. You are growing up not only physically, but you are all strong in the Lord. I am proud of you.

Acknowledgments

I want to thank those who have been an absolute inspiration in my life. Throughout the years it is easy to see where they have had a significant impact.

First, to my God and Savior, Jesus Christ, who is my source of life. Lord Jesus, you are my best friend. You have been with me since I was a child. Thank you for giving me life by exchanging your strength for my failures. Your overwhelming grace and mercy have overlooked my many faults and flaws. Without you, none of this would be possible. Holy Spirit, thank you for your constant abiding presence that never allows me to stray far from my purpose. You remind me of the great task before me. Your anointing empowers the gifts within that will allow me to fulfill the calling upon my life. Father, thank you for the love you have shown in providing such abundance in my life. I realize that apart from you, I can do nothing. My desire is to walk in holiness before you by faith so that you will be pleased in everything I do.

Second, I want to thank my mom and dad for their encouragement. Through everything, they had the ability to put my interests ahead of their own. My stepparents, Chuck and Grace, for being such a blessing in my life. God bless you.

Third, I want to thank my Pastors throughout the years: Walt Buck, Jim Terry, Leonard White, Al Batterson, Dale Maw, James Gilbert, Duane French and Ed Nordby. Each of you in your own way contributed significantly to the Pastor I am today.

Fourth, to the following ministries that have significantly helped mold my knowledge about the Lord Jesus Christ. The Assemblies of God, Kenneth Copeland, Kenneth Hagin, Fred Price, Norvel Hayes, Lester Sumrall, Charles Capps and so many more. Thank God for all of you.

Fifth, all of my ministerial friends whose knowledge, wisdom, insight and ministries have also been a resource in my life. Kevin and Sheila Gerald, Steve and Danielle Hage, Ruckins and Roslyn McKinley, Glenn and Sherilyn Miller, Jim and Rosie Parker, Rick and Linda Sharkey, Casey and Wendy Treat, and of course all of our ILM friends. God bless you all.

Finally, I want to thank the many people who have supported my wife and I in ministry and especially our church family and staff. Eric and Rebecca Hawkins; Eric, you have always been there partner. You and your lovely wife deserve the best! I am committed to you. Brek and Trishelle Ruiz; thank you for your vision and constant reminder of the generation God has allowed us to Pastor. Ron and Charity Doyl; may God exceed your greatest dreams and expectations. Thanks for being servants. Tom and Donna Sanders; thank you for your loyalty and service. I am blessed to have you as friends. Scottie and Shelly Branson; what can I say? You have been such a tremendous blessing and asset to Kim and I personally and in ministry. God bless you abundantly! LaShund and Kadeesha; I love you dearly. Thanks for keeping the dream alive. You both light up the atmosphere with possibility. James and Tammy; thanks for allowing each other to follow the call of their heart without question. Tammy, your daily assistance is such a blessing. Thanks for having the courage to stand in the face of opposition knowing you are fulfilling God's purpose. Thomas and Kerry; thanks for your dependability. Stay strong in the Lord. Kim and I are blessed to Pastor the greatest people in the world . . . God's people. Craig and Ann Swenson, Bob and Zanthe Kenney—the secret faith behind this project. God bless you for your vision and ability to see beyond the natural. A special thanks to Ken and Annette Wren and Award Winning Photography for the cover photo. Last but not least of all, Spokane Faith Center, your love and support have made it possible for me to stay in the presence of the Lord and together we are fulfilling our destiny in Him. God bless you all!

Endorsements

In a subject where all too often a diluted message has produced a deluded people, Lonny Bingle has struck a balance that will enable believers to win in the arena of Spiritual warfare.

Dr. Jim Reeve
Faith Community Church
West Covina, California

❑   ❑   ❑

Thank you Lonny for bringing spiritual warfare out of the heavenlies and into our everyday lives, where it belongs. I recommend this book for every believer. Great job!

Pastor Kevin Gerald
Covenant Celebration Church
Tacoma, Washington

❑   ❑   ❑

Lonny has written great insights for "true Spirituality" and warfare. You will be encouraged and empowered for success in life as you read and study. Anytime we can have "practical" and "spiritual," we know it will be good.

Pastor Casey Treat
Christian Faith Center
Seattle, Washington

❑   ❑   ❑

A fresh book . . . A joy to read. It is simple and practical with great insight into the real battles of life. I really enjoyed it!

Pastor Robert J. Koke
Shoreline Christian Center
Austin, Texas

❑   ❑   ❑

Now we know that the warfare is not between God and Satan (what an insult to God) but between our ears. Dr. Lonny Bingle has taken his earned credentials as a psychologist and a charismatic pastor to show us and grow us through the spiritual warfare maze that has left more hype than hope. Lonny is my friend and more importantly is a friend to truth. Read and rejoice! I wholeheartedly recommend *Enemy in the Mirror.*

Pastor Phil Munsey
Life Church
Mission Viejo, CA

❏   ❏   ❏

I like Dr. Bingle's approach: simple, biblical and to the point. It reminds me of Jesus. Dr. Bingle brings simplicity to an often confused and misunderstood arena of Christian experience. Prepare for a change in the way you think about "Spiritual Warfare." This book could change your life.

John S. Moon
Lord of All Ministries
San Diego, California

❏   ❏   ❏

Dr. Lonny Bingle gives an inspired declaration, defusing the erroneous teaching imbedded in the belief today surrounding the many myths of spiritual warfare. As I have ministered in hundreds of churches around the world I have found far too many believers in a repetition of impotent traditionalism and neglected truth. Reading this book seriously and thoughtfully will help you appropriate God's Word in your life. I believe this book was given by "Divine Insight." I recommend the book *Enemy in the Mirror* unequivocally!

Edward J. Windsor
United Kingdom

❏   ❏   ❏

Enemy in the Mirror is a must read for the new breed. The insight that Dr. Lonny Bingle brings forth is not only powerful but refreshes as well. It causes you to have a longing and hunger for more of God's word. The examples used by Pastor Lonny make it easy for all to grasp and bring spiritual warfare out of this place where only the "deep" can go, but bring it into simplicity and relevancy to the individual believer. I believe that the truth revealed in *Enemy in the Mirror* and applied personally will set many people free from religious mind-sets.

Ruckins McKinley, D.D.
Generation of Demonstration
Irvine, California

❏   ❏   ❏

One of the great mistakes Christians make is the misapplication of Truth. This mistake has robbed many Christians of both maturity and victory in the battles of life. Dr. Lonny Bingle has done an excellent job exposing this common weakness in the Christian's response to the problems and adversity they face. I wholeheartedly recommend this book as an essential tool in laying a foundation for a successful Christian life in the midst of much confusion.

Glenn F. Miller
Bold Lion Ministries
Pensacola, Florida

Foreword

Over the past several years, there's been a topic called spiritual warfare that's been preached about all over the world. It's been talked about in depth in some cities and hardly at all in others. Either way, it has caused a great stir of curiosity in the minds and hearts of believers. We have wanted to know what it means, if we're supposed to be warriors, if we're missing out in our daily Christian lives if we don't fully understand or participate in it. What really is spiritual warfare? How do we "do it?"

Get ready, because Dr. Lonny Bingle will help you understand what spiritual warfare is and how to win the battle against the devil in your daily walk with the Lord. Simple to understand and easy to read, with many enlightening scriptures, this book is an answer for those of us who have prayed for clarification of this important subject.

My favorite thought from this book is when Dr. Bingle says, "True spiritual warfare is not the ability to control demons but to control ourselves." Because, most of the important battles we face will be waged within ourselves. We must renew our minds with the Word of God.

Who gives you more trouble than you? Have you felt like Dwight L. Moody when he said, "I have never met a man who gave me more trouble than myself?" The first and best victory is to conquer yourself.

The basic problem most people have is that they are doing nothing to solve their basic problem. This problem is: they build a case against themselves. They are their own worst enemy.

I know that as you read this book you will discover how to be truly free! Praise God.

John Mason

Preface

I have noticed during the course of my life and several years of being involved in the ministry that many people seem to overspiritualize "spiritual warfare." The term itself engages the minds of people into a mystic realm of demonic forces: A spiritual army waiting to terrorize and possess the lives of men. A force so powerful that only the elite in God can understand and confront them. An enemy so unpredictable that only personal experiences can truly bring one into the full understanding of his operations. In the midst of fantasies such as these, many have given Satan a position that is virtually unstoppable.

I have witnessed the deliverance ministries of the sixties, the revival of deliverance in the eighties, and I am convinced that we are entering into a renewed interest in the field of deliverance in this new millennium. We must not be ignorant of the devil's schemes, but to be effective we must focus on true biblical deliverance. The book of Ephesians gives us God's blueprint for life which will allow us to be fully prepared to fulfill the deliverance needs of this generation.

Because of the nature of this subject, I encourage every reader to compare and prove all things according to scripture. The personal experiences and revelation of others should never be the basis for one's personal faith. Too many books concerning spiritual warfare have been written sincerely but inaccurately from personal experiences. People have accepted the factual deception of the enemy concerning his kingdom as truth and have elevated demonic testimony to the level of scriptural authority. Subtle deceptions have been turned into doctrine. Many who have given themselves over to such distractions can tell you more about the devil and his supposed operations than they can about the Lord Jesus Christ and the power of the cross. They have positioned themselves in their own minds as superior to the average believer because of their so-called deliverance ministries.

God bless you for your interest in spiritual warfare and true biblical deliverance. I believe that we can make a difference in our generation. I believe we can be the forcefully advancing church of the new millennium. I believe that we will be stronger together when we fully understand the impact we have when we operate according to God's word.

CHAPTER ONE

The Arena of Spiritual Warfare

My interest in spiritual warfare really began in October of 1981. I was recently discharged from the United States Navy and had just begun to work with the youth at the church I had been a member of for years. One Sunday evening I was given the opportunity to preach. I chose Ephesians 6:12 as my text and preached what I thought was the message of the century. I knew I was God's gift to the ministry and that I was destined for greatness in God. Little did I know that it would take a little ninety-pound girl to bring me back to reality.

In June of the following year, I was in my office as youth Pastor. I had an appointment with a young lady that I had led to the Lord a few months earlier. I had been studying what I thought was spiritual warfare and was convinced that she was possessed. I had the room set up just right. I had my intercessors (two friends who were construction workers with good hearts) present to engage in "spiritual warfare." When she arrived, all hell broke loose. We had demons naming themselves, we tried to hold her still, she screamed, we screamed, everybody screamed, we were engaged! Then without warning she simply picked up my intercessors with one hand and threw them off of her. This ninety-pound young girl had just picked up a 6'2" friend of mine who weighed in at 220 pounds and threw him off. Now we were binding everything (from a distance of course).

Many things happened that day and we left with a feeling of accomplishment. That young lady probably stayed free from demonic influence for at least four hours. Needless to say, we didn't know as much as we thought and I soon realized I knew very little about true spiritual warfare. Like so many believers, I thought that intercession and casting out demons encompassed the entire field of spiritual warfare. Now I recognize that over the years we have developed a philosophy of spiritual warfare by extrapolating the scripture, listening to the deception of the enemy, combining it with personal experiences, and then changing it into doctrine.

> **". . . over the years we have developed a philosophy of spiritual warfare by extrapolating the scripture, listening to the deception of the enemy, combining it with personal experiences, and then changing it into doctrine."**

Paul instructed Timothy to remember the prophetic utterances (divinely inspired **word of God**, 2 Peter 1:21) which had been spoken over his life. By holding onto faith (which cometh by hearing the **word of God,** Romans 10:17), and a good conscience (a mind renewed by the **word of God,** Romans 12:1-2), he could war a good warfare! Notice what I have highlighted. True spiritual warfare comes from a focus on the word of God (Jesus) and not Satan, devils or demonic activities.

The new covenant only mentions warfare or a form of it ten times and only one of those could be construed to deal with demonic entities.

Who goeth a **warfare** *any time at his own charges?*

1 Corinthians 9:7a

I therefore so run, not as uncertainly; so **fight** *I, not as one that beateth the air:* **But I keep under my body, and bring it into subjection:** *lest that by any means, when I have preached to others, I myself should be a castaway.*

1 Corinthians 9:26-27

For though we walk in the flesh, we do not **war** *after the flesh: (For the weapons of our warfare are not carnal, but mighty through God to the* **pulling down of strong holds;)** **Casting down imaginations, and every high thing that exalteth itself against the knowledge of God, and bringing into captivity every thought** *to the obedience of Christ; And having in a readiness to revenge all disobedience, when your obedience is fulfilled.*

2 Corinthians 10:3-6

This charge I commit unto thee, son Timothy, according to the prophecies which went before on thee, that thou by them mightest **war** *a* **good** **warfare; Holding faith, and a good conscience;** *which some having put away concerning faith have made shipwreck:*

1 Timothy 1:18-19

For we **wrestle** *not against flesh and blood, but* **against principalities, against powers, against the rulers** *of the darkness of this world, against spiritual wickedness in high places.*

Ephesians 6:12

Fight the good fight of faith, *lay hold on eternal life, whereunto thou art also called, and hast professed a good profession before many witnesses.*

1 Timothy 6:12

No man that **warreth entangleth himself** *with the affairs of this life; that he may please him who hath chosen him to be a soldier.*

2 Timothy 2:4

I have **fought a good fight,** *I have finished my course, I have* **kept the faith:**

2 Timothy 4:7

From whence come **wars and fightings** *among you?* **Come they not hence, even of your lusts** *that war in your members?*

James 4:1

Dearly beloved, I beseech you as strangers and pilgrims, abstain from **fleshly lusts, which war against the soul;**

1 Peter 2:11

Notice that the majority of the scriptures dealing with spiritual warfare are referring to renewing the mind and dealing with the flesh, not contending with demonic entities. Therefore, I would submit that true spiritual warfare is:

"The ability to appropriate and enact the word of God in any given situation or circumstance."

If that means changing the way we think and act to line up to the word of God, great! If it means casting out a devil that is standing in the way of fulfilling the plans and purposes of God, great!

> **"We must not become intrigued with the mystique of the demonic realm allowing that perspective to take our eyes off of God and His word."**

We must not become intrigued with the mystique of the demonic realm allowing that perspective to take our eyes off of God and His word. True spiritual warfare and deliverance will be 90% renewing the mind and 10% dealing in the arena of devils. As believers, we have inverted that ratio and made Satan the focus of our warfare.

> ***Fight the good fight of faith,*** *lay hold on eternal life, whereunto thou art also called, and hast professed a good profession before many witnesses.*
>
> *1 Timothy 6:12*

The good fight of faith is what we need to concern ourselves with. Paul told the church at Rome that faith comes by hearing the word of God.

So then faith cometh by hearing, and hearing by the word of God.

Romans 10:17

Therefore, the majority of spiritual warfare is fighting the good fight of faith. Standing for our holiness when we want to sin. Standing for our healing when we feel sick. Standing for our prosperity in the midst of a financial crisis. Standing for our families in the midst of every day pressures. Standing when there seems like there is no reason left to stand.

*Wherefore take unto you the whole armour of God, that ye may be able to with**stand** in the evil day, and having done all, to **stand**. **Stand** therefore . . .*

Ephesians 6:13-14a

Those who are truly involved in deliverance are showing people how to **stand** day by day according to the word of God and not just giving them a spiritual "feel good" or demonic sideshow. There will be appropriate times for casting out devils. First we must concentrate on the tasks that lay before us in true spiritual warfare which consists of renewing our minds to the word of God. We must demand from ourselves the diligence to allow the word of God to have a complete work in us.

Study to shew thyself approved unto God, *a workman that needeth not to be ashamed,* **rightly dividing the word of truth.**

2 Timothy 2:15

The Apostle Paul instructed a young minister by the name of Timothy to study in order to become an approved workman unto God. By the same token, I believe that a lack of study can cause one to be an unapproved workman unto God. Both are working unto God. Both love God. Both are loved by God. Both are sincere, but only one has God's approval. There are no shortcuts to becoming a skilled laborer in the kingdom of God. We must study God's word in order to understand His will. The word *"study"* as used above literally means three things. It will take time, effort, and consistency if we are to become approved unto God. You must pay a price demonstrated by a completely abandoned lifestyle of commitment.

My intent is to allow the word of God to become champion and set aside the personal experiences upon which personal doctrine and conviction have become entrenched. We must realize that our experiences, however real, are not and must never be the basis for faith and action.

> **But the natural man receiveth not the things of the Spirit of God:** *for they are foolishness unto him: neither can he know them, because* **they are spiritually discerned.**
>
> *1 Corinthians 2:14*

Many have been deceived because they have taken the knowledge and experiences of others and have not proven all things according to scripture themselves.

> *These (in Berea) were more noble than those in Thessalonica, in that they* **received the word with all readiness of**

mind, and searched the scriptures daily, whether those things were so.

Acts 17:11

If you were to simply take this book at face value without searching diligently to prove the things I write to you, **you become a candidate for deception.** Notice, however, the attitude of the Bereans. They received the word with all readiness of mind . . . whether those things were so. They did not search the scriptures daily to prove the speaker wrong, but to see if what was written was in agreement with the truth of God. Such diligence brought them into an understanding of the word of God and a commendation by the Holy Spirit. Their understanding produced faith wherewith they could fight the good fight of faith. Deception would not have found an easy resting place in the believers at Berea because of their firm foundation in the word of God.

We must have a strong foundation in the word of God if we are going to properly understand and operate in the arena of true spiritual warfare. Appropriating and enacting the word of God while facing any situation or circumstance is the mark of a mature warrior of the Lord. If we are to excel in the arena of spiritual warfare, we must be able to differentiate between facts and truth, appearances and revelation, experiences and the word of God. With these thoughts in mind, let us explore the biblical deliverance according to the word of God.

Keys to Remember

The Arena of Spiritual Warfare

❑   Personal experiences should never be converted into doctrine.

❑   True spiritual warfare comes from a focus on the word of God (Jesus) and not Satan, devils or demonic activities.

❑   True spiritual warfare is: **"The ability to appropriate and enact the word of God in any given situation or circumstance."**

❑   True spiritual warfare and deliverance will be 90% renewing the mind and 10% dealing in the arena of devils.

❑   The majority of spiritual warfare is fighting the good fight of faith.

CHAPTER TWO

Truth vs. Fact

Early on in ministry I was heavily involved in street ministry. One Friday night I was in downtown Spokane, Washington, looking for a vagrant man that had recently been born again. I had been taking him to church where he had been baptized. He had not missed a single service until one Wednesday night. Knowing that he had been an alcoholic, I went downtown to find him. I knew which hangouts had been his and so I went back into the tavern where I was sure he must be. As soon as I walked in, the bartender looked at me and began to scream, "You get out of here! We don't want your kind in here!" I had never met him but I knew I had stirred up something in the spirit realm. I looked at him and calmly said, "You have come against a man of God and now this establishment will fold within six months." That tavern closed up within the following six months and is now a Christian teen center.

Well, wouldn't you know it. One of the deacons at my church happened to be downtown and saw me walk into the bar. The next thing I knew, I had to explain why I was frequenting a bar. The fact was that I had gone into a bar. The truth was, I had gone in there to witness and to bring a man out that was struggling. What my deacon had seen was correct but it was only factual and not truth. Such experiences as this led me to the conclusion that we must always be careful of a half-truth because we might have the wrong half. It would have been very easy for me to have been fired over that situation had fact won out over truth. The same is true with our faith.

I grew up in the church and now realize that much of what we believed was based on our experiences (facts leading to tradition) rather than truth (revelation which comes from God's word). The church readily accepted such facts as truth, not discerning the difference, and have, therefore, allowed the traditions of men to destroy the faith of God.

> *But he answered and said unto them, Why do ye also* **transgress the commandment** *of God* **by your tradition?**
> *Matthew 15:3*

> **For laying aside the commandment of God, ye hold the tradition of men . . .**
> *Mark 7:8a*

> *And he said unto them, Full well* **ye reject the commandment of God, that ye may keep your own tradition.**
> *Mark 7:9*

> **Making the word of God of none effect through your tradition . . .**
> *Mark 7:13*

> *Beware lest any man* **spoil you** *through philosophy and vain deceit,* **after the tradition of men,** *after the rudiments of the world, and not after Christ.*
> *Colossians 2:8*

> *Forasmuch as ye know that ye were not redeemed with corruptible things, as silver and gold, from your* **vain conversation received by tradition** *from your fathers;*
>
> *1 Peter 1:18*

Please understand, not all traditions are wrong. Paul wrote to the church in Thessalonica and told them about acceptable traditions.

> *Therefore, brethren, stand fast, and* **hold the traditions** *which ye have been taught, whether* **by word, or our epistle.**
>
> *2 Thessalonians 2:15*

> *Now we command you, brethren, in the name of our Lord Jesus Christ, that ye withdraw yourselves from every brother that walketh disorderly, and not after* **the tradition which he received of us.**
>
> *2 Thessalonians 3:6*

So what is the difference? Very simply put, traditions that are solidly based upon the word of God and not our personal biases are scriptural. Traditions that come as the result of our experiences and emotions should not be elevated to the level of scriptural authority. Such traditions will hinder us from receiving what God has for us by generating hollow doctrines. Most likely those doctrines will be contrary to the will of God.

Many of our ideas and biblical concepts have been birthed out of personal experiences or events that occur only once in the word of God. Some of these experiences and events have been turned into doctrine improperly. For example, Jesus healed a man by spitting on the ground, making mud, and then smearing it in his eyes. It is true that this happened (John 9:6), however, it is not a truth that we should turn this event into doctrine since it occurred only once. We should not establish a new movement of the, "Spiritual Mud Slingers for the Recovery of Sight." Jesus walked on the water, but we should not enter into our sanctuaries weekly and try to walk across the baptismal. Jesus asked a devil to

> **"We should not turn single Bible events (facts) into biblical doctrine (truth)."**

name himself, and yet we should not turn that into doctrine either. Some have experienced wild demonic manifestations while helping someone who is under demonic influence (myself included), but none of this should become doctrinal.

There are principles that we learn from each of these events and circumstances, however, we should not turn single events (facts) into biblical doctrine (truth). Many things are recorded in the Bible and they are absolutely true (factual), but they are not truth. The children of Israel wandered in the wilderness for forty years (Numbers 32:13), that's true (factual). But it would not be truth that God desires you to wander for forty years looking for your promised land. It is true (factual) that God used a donkey to speak to Balaam (Numbers 22:28), but it would not be truth for that animal to be the only true oracle of God. It is true (factual) that King David committed adultery (2 Samuel 11:3-4) and had a man murdered (2 Samuel 11:15), but those are not the actions necessary to have a heart after God (1 Samuel 13:14;

1 Kings 11:4). It is true (factual) that the walls of Jericho fell by marching around them thirteen times at the direction and plan of the Lord (Joshua 6), but it is not truth that having a Jericho march in your church will cause the walls of your problem to fall. It is true (factual) that Jesus commanded the demons in a demoniac to name themselves (Luke 8:30), but that does not mean this is the pattern (truth) for deliverance.

Please understand, everything in the Bible is true and has a practical purpose. God considered it important enough to have it recorded by men under the direct inspiration of the Holy Spirit. But just because it is recorded (true) in the Bible does not make it a pattern (truth) to follow. Many things recorded in the word of God were recorded to show us the failures of men and how to avoid them. Their failures were not patterns for us to follow. Truth is something we pattern are lives after. What is true is what we learn from. Experiences are true and we can learn from them, but we must not turn them into truth or doctrine!

Why is it so important that we learn the difference between truth and fact? Our ability to stand strong in spiritual warfare (the ability to appropriate and enact the word of God in any given situation or circumstance) will be dependent on our ability to accurately discern and discriminate between fact and truth. For example, it may be true (factual) that you have been diagnosed with some disease, but the truth is, "with his stripes you were healed." If you are unable to discern between the report you receive in the natural and the supernatural law you are to live by, you may live in the diagnosis you have received and even die from the disease. That is not God's will for you, but a lack of knowledge can lead to captivity, then destruction.

Therefore **my people are gone into captivity, because they have no knowledge:**

Isaiah 5:13a

My **people are destroyed for lack of knowledge: because thou hast rejected knowledge, I will also reject thee,** *thou shalt be no priest to me: seeing thou hast forgotten the law of thy God, I will also forget thy children.*

Hosea 4:6

The thief does not come except to steal, and to kill, and to destroy. *I have come that they may have life, and that they may have it more abundantly.*

John 10:10 (NKJ)

Do not be deceived. Satan's only goal is to steal, kill and destroy. *Satan doesn't even come unless he is going to steal, kill, and destroy.* We must understand the tool that allows us to operate in discernment and disarm the enemy is the word of God. Ignorance of the word allows Satan to gain ground in our lives when we are trying to stand firm. Many of the problems people face become tragic because they lack the knowledge of the word of God to stand firm. One of the reasons that I have put so much scripture in this book is because I realize the value of supporting everything we believe with the word of God. What excuse will we offer to the Lord for not obtaining the knowledge we needed to stand firm? So much is available to us which would enable us to grow up into Him. We really do not have any excuses for a lack of knowledge. The Apostle Paul wrote the church at Ephesus warning us against giving the devil a foothold.

Neither give place to the devil.

Ephesians 4:27

and do not give the devil a foothold.

Ephesians 4:27 (NIV)

These references basically mean that we cannot give the devil a little room in a large house. Many times everything seems to be going well but we refuse to deal with one area in our lives. Maybe an area of unforgiveness, maybe some secret sin, whatever it is, we leave a door open to the enemy and push truth away from our lives. Those who lead a life of warfare realize the necessity for a consistent stand in the word of God.

One of the problems I see today is that we stand long enough to bring us to a point of comfort. Once we have achieved our level of complacency, then we no longer feel

> **"Our ability to stand strong in spiritual warfare will be dependent on our ability to accurately discern and discriminate between fact and truth."**

the urgency to press for the new level in God. Many people believe they are fulfilling the calling that God has placed in their life, when in fact they are fulfilling a delusion they are willing to accept generated by their own level of comfort. Then, when troubles arise, they realize how inadequate their faith really is and begin to blame their situation on the devil and enter into "spiritual warfare."

Unfortunately, the warfare they enter into is not true warfare. It is a pseudo-spiritual warfare that eases the convictions of their mind. They refuse to hear the voice of the spirit which is dealing with truth and they listen to the voice of soulish warfare dealing with fact. Most of the time they end up in more bondage than when they began. We must remain steadfast in the things of God realizing that everything in our lives is dependent upon His word.

The Apostle Paul gave the perfect instructions to the church at Ephesus for true spiritual warfare. His instructions gave explicit details for dealing in principles of truth. We need to push beyond situations and circumstances (facts) and press into the word of God (truth) so we can fulfill God's divine plans and purposes for our lives. I pray that truth will rule supreme and we may mature past the point of being driven by the facts that constantly rise to challenge our position in Christ; that we might be able to accurately discern the truth that promotes us to new levels in God. Let us take a look at the truth we can learn from Ephesus: the city, its people, and the letter directed to them by the Apostle Paul.

Keys to Remember

Truth vs. Fact

☐   The traditions of men destroy the faith of God.

☐   We should not turn single Bible events (facts) into biblical doctrine (truth).

☐   Satan's only goal is to steal, kill and destroy. *Satan doesn't even come unless he is going to steal, kill, and destroy.*

☐   We need to push beyond situations and circumstances (facts) and press into the word of God (truth) so we can fulfill God's divine plans and purposes for our lives.

CHAPTER THREE

Ministering to the Heart

Remember that first sermon I told you about where I thought I was God's gift to ministry. Well, in the midst of that sermon I quoted Isaiah 58 concerning true fasting. I read verse eight wrong.

> *Then shall thy light break forth as the morning, and thine health shall spring forth speedily: and thy righteousness shall go before thee; the glory of the LORD shall be thy **rereward**.*
>
> *Isaiah 58:8*

I read that last word as re-reward instead of rere-ward. Well, I made a huge point of how God would reward us again (re-reward) for our diligence in Him. I didn't realize it meant that he would cover our hind side as we went through life. I was very sincere in what I preached, but I was sincerely wrong. After that embarrassing moment, I realized that I had better get a thorough understanding of the text before I tried to preach on it. I believe the same principle would be wise for us as we briefly discuss the book of Ephesians.

Ephesus was a vitally important city on the west coast of Asia Minor. It was the most favorable seaport in the province of Asia and the most important trade center west of Tarsus. Ephesus was the largest city in the province with a reported population of approximately 300,000 people. Ephesus was also a cultural center containing a theater that seated an estimated 25,000 people. A main thoroughfare, some 35 meters (105 feet) wide, ran from the theater to the harbor, at each end of which stood an impressive gate. The thoroughfare was flanked on each side by rows of columns 15 meters (50 feet) deep. Behind these columns were baths, gymnasiums, and impressive buildings.

Last but not at all least, Ephesus was a religious center. The Temple of Artemis (or Diana, according to her Roman name) at Ephesus ranked as one of the Seven Wonders of the Ancient World. As the twin sister of Apollo and the daughter of Zeus, Artemis was known variously as the moon goddess, the goddess of hunting, and the patroness of young girls. The temple at Ephesus housed the multi-breasted image of Artemis which was reputed to have come directly from Zeus.

*The city clerk quieted the crowd and said: "Men of **Ephesus, doesn't all the world know that the city of Ephesus is the guardian of the temple of the great Artemis** and of her image, which fell from heaven?*

Acts 19:35 (NIV)

*And when the city clerk had quieted the crowd, he said: "Men of Ephesus, what man is there who does not know that the city of the Ephesians is temple guardian of the great goddess Diana, and of **the image which fell down from Zeus?***

Acts 19:35 (NKJ)

Here in the midst of a polytheistic environment, the Apostle Paul helps to establish a church that will be extremely significant in the history of Christianity. This history begins about A. D. 50, perhaps as a result of the efforts of Priscilla and Aquila.

> *After this,* **Paul** *left Athens and went to Corinth. There he* **met a Jew named Aquila,** *a native of Pontus, who had recently come from Italy* **with his wife Priscilla,** *because Claudius had ordered all the Jews to leave Rome. Paul went to see them, and because he was a tentmaker as they were, he stayed and worked with them . . .*
>
> *. . . Paul stayed on in Corinth for some time. Then* **he left** *the brothers and sailed for Syria,* **accompanied by Priscilla and Aquila.** *Before he sailed, he had his hair cut off at Cenchrea because of a vow he had taken.* **They arrived at Ephesus, where Paul left Priscilla and Aquila.** *He himself went into the synagogue and reasoned with the Jews. When they asked him to spend more time with them, he declined. But as* **he left,** *he promised, "I will come back if it is God's will." Then he* **set sail from Ephesus.**
>
> *Acts 18:1-3; 18-21* (NIV)

Paul then returned to Ephesus about A. D. 52, establishing a resident ministry for the better part of three years. During the apostle's ministry there, it was reported that "all who dwelt in Asia heard the word of the Lord Jesus" (Acts 19:10). He would bring his knowledge and anointing to teach during the hot midday hours in the lecture hall of Tyrannus.

> *So be on your guard! Remember that* **for three years I never stopped** *warning each of you night and day with tears.*
>
> *Acts 20:31* (NIV)

*But some of them became obstinate; they refused to believe and publicly maligned the Way. So Paul left them. **He** took the disciples with him and **had discussions daily in the lecture hall of Tyrannus.***

Acts 19:9 (NIV)

So strong was his influence, that the founding of the churches in Lycus River valley at Laodicea, Hierapolis, and Colossae were probably the direct result of his teaching.

Paul's ministry at Ephesus had such an impact upon the community, that the silversmith's league, which fashioned souvenirs of the temple, feared the preaching of the gospel would undermine the great temple of Artemis. As a result, one of the silversmiths named Demetrius stirred up a riot against him (Acts 19:24-41).

"Before the apostle Paul mentioned anything about 'spiritual warfare' to the church at Ephesus, he ministered to their hearts, edifying them in Christ Jesus."

As you can read, the Apostle Paul was a man who experienced many challenges in the city of Ephesus. Not only natural opposition, but spiritual. Demonic activity was readily seen here. Notice the seven sons of Sceva (Acts 19). But Paul never allowed his circumstances to dictate his destiny. He knew how to appropriate the word of God in every situation. He understood true warfare. It was under such opposition that he introduced the believers in Ephesus to the baptism with the Holy Spirit. No matter what the need was,

Paul was instant in and out of season and allowed the word of God to rule supreme through his life.

No wonder the Holy Spirit decided to give such great teaching on spiritual warfare to the church at Ephesus. They were faced with a culture that was steeped in religious traditions and demonic activity. In the midst of this environment, God chose to reveal His heart concerning deliverance. Paul did not chase after demonic entities, he strove to fulfill the plan of God. When those who were possessed tried to hinder his purpose in Ephesus, he simply cast the devils out in the name of Jesus. So rich would this area be with the gospel, that the Apostle John decides to make Ephesus his home until his death towards the end of the first century.

After Paul departed from Ephesus, he left Timothy there to combat false teaching.

> *As I urged you when I went into Macedonia, stay there in Ephesus so that you may command certain men not to teach false doctrines any longer nor to devote themselves to myths and endless genealogies. These promote controversies rather than God's work—which is by faith.*
>
> 1 Timothy 1:3-4 (NIV)

> *I charge thee therefore before God, and the Lord Jesus Christ, who shall judge the quick and the dead at his appearing and his kingdom; Preach the word; be instant in season, out of season; reprove, rebuke, exhort with all longsuffering and doctrine. For the time will come when they will not endure sound doctrine; but after their own lusts shall they heap to themselves teachers, having itching ears; And they shall turn away their ears from the truth, and shall be turned unto fables. But*

watch thou in all things, endure afflictions, do the work of an evangelist, make full proof of thy ministry.

2 Timothy 4:1-5

Keep watch over yourselves and all the flock of which the Holy Spirit has made you overseers. Be shepherds of the church of God, which he bought with his own blood. I know that after I leave, savage wolves will come in among you and will not spare the flock. Even from your own number men will arise and distort the truth in order to draw away disciples after them.

Acts 20:28-30 (NIV)

The Apostle Paul warned of false doctrines that would arise. Unfortunately, it would rise among the ranks of Christian Pastors and leaders. I truly believe that one of those doctrines of devils was a demonic testimony of how to operate in spiritual warfare. Much of that mentality still prevails today and we must bring a balance to this subject in the body of Christ.

The one verse that has often been referenced concerning warfare with demonic entities is found in Ephesians chapter six. Without debating the merits of this verse, let's assume it refers to demonic entities. What amazes me is the fact that we want to take the "finally" of chapter six and make it the "first" rule of doctrine in our stance on spiritual warfare. I would submit that we need to take a look at what preceeds the "finally" before we truly understand what the Holy Spirit was trying to reveal. What did He have to say before he dealt with the arena of wrestling with principalities, powers, rulers and spiritual wickedness?

Before the apostle Paul mentioned anything about "spiritual warfare" to the church at Ephesus, he ministered to their hearts, edifying them in Christ Jesus. The first three chapters in the book of Ephesians dealt mainly with who they were in Christ. The last three chapters dealt with their responsibilities in Christ. The truth that Paul wrote under the inspiration of the Holy Spirit for the church at Ephesus is still truth for the church of today.

Keys to Remember

Ministering to the Heart

❑   In Ephesus, in the midst of a polytheistic environment, the apostle Paul helps to establish a church that
will be extremely significant in the history of
Christianity.

❑   During the apostle Paul's ministry in Ephesus, it was
reported that "all who dwelt in Asia heard the word
of the Lord Jesus" (Acts 19:10).

❑   We should not allow circumstances to dictate our destiny.

❑   Beware of false doctrines that may arise even within
the ranks of the ministry.

❑   We must not take the "finally" of chapter six and
make it the "first" rule of doctrine in our stance on
spiritual warfare.

❑   The truth that Paul wrote under the inspiration of the
Holy Spirit for the church at Ephesus is still truth for
the church of today.

CHAPTER FOUR

Knowing God's Nature

Early on in my deliverance ministry, I studied everything I could get my hands on concerning the devil and his operations. I could tell you everything you would ever want to know about Satan and his devices. I mean after all, we are not to be ignorant of the way the devil operates, right? Unfortunately, in my sincerity to follow God, I had missed the most important aspect of deliverance. My relationship with Jesus! Devils don't run because I know about them. They run when they know I know Jesus. We should understand this from the example of the seven sons of Sceva in Ephesians chapter nineteen. It still amazes me how many people are just like I was. They can tell me more about the devil and his operations than they can tell me about Jesus.

In his letter to the church at Ephesus, the apostle Paul reminds them of the things that he taught. In the beginning of the book we have a beautiful example of intercessory prayer. A prayer that Paul prayed over the faithful in Christ Jesus. A prayer that is just as alive for us today. Please note that the book of Ephesians was not written as a manual for conquering demons. It wasn't even written to direct our attention to demons. Paul wanted them to see four things *about God*. So he requested wisdom and revelation to enlighten their understanding. The Holy Spirit inspired him to record his words so we could learn from them today.

For this reason, ever since I heard about your faith in the Lord Jesus and your love for all the saints, I have not stopped giving thanks for you, remembering you in my prayers. **I keep asking that** the **God** of our Lord Jesus Christ, the glorious Father, **may give you the Spirit of wisdom and revelation, so that you may know him better. I pray also that the eyes of your heart may be enlightened in order that you may know the hope to which he has called you, the riches of his glorious inheritance in the saints, and his incomparably great power for us who believe.** *That power is like the working of his mighty strength, he exerted in Christ when he raised him from the dead and seated him at his right hand in the heavenly realms, far above all rule and authority, power and dominion, and every title that can be given, not only in the present age but also in the one to come. And God placed all things under his feet and appointed him to be head over everything for the church, which is his body, the fullness of him who fills everything in every way.*

Ephesians 1:15-23 (NIV)

First, he wanted us to "know Him" (God) better. If we read through the book of Ephesians and only see warfare and devils, we have missed what I believe is a vital key to understanding the heart of the writer and the Holy Spirit. Paul's desire for this city that had been bound by idolatry and witchcraft was not a seek and cast out mission against demons, but how to know God. He realized that as you draw near to God, he draws near to you.

Draw nigh to God, and he will draw nigh to you . . .

James 4:8a

If we realize who we are in Him, then the warfare we fight (the good fight of faith) is much simpler. God is the word. Jesus was the word personified. The Holy Spirit (the Spirit of truth) is responsible to reveal and direct us to the word bringing all things to our remembrance.

> *Howbeit when he,* **the Spirit of truth,** *is come, he will guide you into all truth: for he shall not speak of himself; but whatsoever he shall hear, that shall he speak: and he will shew you things to come.* **He shall glorify me: for he shall receive of mine, and shall shew it unto you.**
>
> *John 16:13-14*

> **But the Comforter, which is the Holy Ghost,** *whom the Father will send in my name,* **he shall teach you all things, and bring all things to your remembrance, whatsoever I have said unto you.**
>
> *John 14:26*

Should the need ever arise where we need to cast out devils, we will do so not because of our understanding of devils, but because of our understanding of God and His word.

Second, he wanted us to know the "hope" to which he has called us. I have noticed that many who speak of deliverance ministry always talk about the gloom over a city; the ruling demonic spirits over a region, the dark strongholds that are present. Now that really builds hope. Paul said, he wants you to know the *hope* God has provided for you. Not the doom and gloom, not the power of Satan. No, we were to know about God's hope. I understand that there are territorial demons over regions and strongholds in the minds of many, but that should never be our focus. This word "hope" means to have a pleasureful anticipation, an expectation with confidence. Our confidence should be in God. I have said it like this, "There should be an excited confidence that what God has said is truth. A joyful expectation that God will perform everything he has promised. A pleasureful anticipation that our God is moving, right now, on our behalf, even before we see it."

> **"If we read through the book of Ephesians and only see warfare and devils, we have missed what I believe is a vital key to understanding the heart of the writer and the Holy Spirit."**

Peter talked about this kind of hope. He knew that if we carried this hope in us, it would be the catalyst to spreading the gospel of Jesus.

> *But sanctify the Lord God in your hearts: and* **be ready always to give an answer to every man that asketh you a reason of the hope that is in you** *with meekness and fear:*
>
> *1 Peter 3:15*

Peter understood this type of hope. Wherever he went it was evident. The Bible records that those who were brought into his shadow (tangible anointing) were healed.

> *And believers were the more added to the Lord, multitudes both of men and women. Insomuch that they brought forth the sick into the streets, and laid them on beds and couches, that at*

*the least the shadow of Peter passing by might overshadow some
of them.*

Acts 5:14-15

What hope that must have brought to the hearts of people!
How many would have come to believe on Jesus not because a
devil was cast out, but because they saw a loving, caring God?

> **"Our purpose on this planet is to take
> dominion and bring everything into the
> obedience of God's plans and purpose."**

Our purpose on this planet is to take dominion and
bring everything into the obedience of God's plans and purpose. We are to preach the gospel to every creature. The only
time we should be dealing with demonic entities is when they
try to interfere with the purpose God has established in our
lives. Jesus **never** went looking for devils. He simply cast
them out when they came between Him and His purpose.

Third, we were to come to an understanding of "his
glorious inheritance in the saints." What is this inheritance
that belongs to Jesus? There are several different ways to
look at this inheritance. We are his inheritance. We are the
objects that he purchased with his own blood and He has
given to us an inheritance. The blessings of Abraham are
ours now! We will enjoy a new heaven and a new earth as our
eternal home. We are joint-heirs with Jesus!

*Take heed therefore unto yourselves, and to all the flock, over
the which the Holy Ghost hath made you overseers, to **feed***

the church of God, which he hath purchased with his own blood.

Acts 20:28

Christ hath redeemed us *from the curse of the law, being made a curse for us: for it is written, Cursed is every one* **that** *hangeth on a tree:* **That the blessing of Abraham might come on the Gentiles through Jesus Christ; that we might receive the promise of the Spirit through faith.**

Galatians 3:13-14

For ye have not received the spirit of bondage again to fear; but ye have received the Spirit of adoption, whereby we cry, Abba, Father. The Spirit itself beareth witness with our spirit, that **we are the children of God: And if children, then heirs; heirs of God, and joint-heirs with Christ;** *if so be that we suffer with him, that we may be also glorified together.*

Romans 8:15-17

To me this is what is exciting and full of hope. I am not like those in the world without hope. I am a child of God with all the rights and privileges of royalty in the heavenly court. I have a right to come boldly before the throne of God. I have a right to call him daddy. And all of it is because of the cross. There is no demon in hell that can stop my rights or hinder my progress with my Father. Only I can impede and cloud my destiny in Him.

For we are his workmanship, created in Christ Jesus unto good works, *which God hath before ordained* *that we should walk in them. Wherefore* **remember, that ye being in time past** *Gentiles in the flesh, who are called Uncircumcision by that which is called the Circumcision in the flesh made by hands; That at that time ye were without Christ, being aliens from the commonwealth of Israel, and* **strangers from the covenants of promise, having no hope, and without God in the world: But now in Christ Jesus ye who sometimes were far off are made nigh by the blood of Christ.**

Ephesians 2:10-13

Let us therefore come boldly unto the throne of grace, *that we may obtain mercy, and find grace to help in time of need.*

Hebrews 4:16

The hope that I have is not generated by my prowess in religious warfare seeking demons, but in my relationship with my Father. He has given me everything necessary for a prosperous, healthy lifestyle. The more I know about Him, the more I can appropriate and enact His will and purpose in my life. That is true warfare.

Last, Paul wanted us to understand what was "his incomparably great power for us who believe. . . ." We simply need to understand that God has great power and has given us the ability to walk in it. Without it, we can do nothing. With it, we will see the invisible, choose the imperishable, and do the impossible. With these things in mind, let us find out who we are in Christ and how He has positioned us in heavenly realms.

Keys to Remember

Knowing God's Nature

❑ The book of Ephesians was not written as a manual for conquering demons. It wasn't even written to direct our attention to demons.

❑ Paul wanted us to see four things *about God.*

    ❑ First, he wanted us to "know Him" (God) better.

    ❑ Second, he wanted us to know the "hope" to which he has called us.

    ❑ Third, we were to come to an understanding of "his glorious inheritance in the saints."

    ❑ Last, we simply need to understand that God has great power and has given us the ability to walk in it.

❑ There is no demon in hell that can stop my rights or hinder my progress with my Father. Only I can impede and cloud my destiny in Him.

CHAPTER FIVE

Who Am I?

One day I was in a therapy session with a client who was going through a mid-life crisis. This particular individual was looking for help in overcoming many different vices in their life. They were dissatisfied with life and suicidal. They had quit their job, left their spouse, abandoned their children, developed a drug and alcohol problem while looking for contentment in shallow one night stands. We had been together for a few sessions and it was overwhelmingly apparent that they were not struggling with their various vices; they were struggling with who they were. I thought to myself and wondered how many other middle-aged people were going through this same type of introspection, wondering about their identity and purpose in life. How many others were looking for a new wife or husband, changing jobs or trying to regain their youth? How many others were struggling with drugs and alcohol looking for satisfaction only to find emptiness? Then I thought, how many people in the body of Christ still do not know who they are?

The Apostle Paul went to great lengths to show us who we are in Christ. Take a highlighter and go through your Bible and underline everywhere it says "in Him," "in whom," "through whom," etc. This helps us realize what God has done in us through the Lord Jesus Christ. Here is what I have found out through the first few chapters of Ephesians:

❑ We are blessed. 1:3

❑ We are part of God's family. 1:5

❑ All of our mistakes and sin have been forgiven. 1:7

❑ God wants to reveal his will and purpose for our lives. 1:9

❑ Our entire life belongs to God. 1:11

❑ Everything Jesus has is at our disposal. 1:13

❑ The Holy Spirit has marked us with a seal for God. 1:13

❑ We have a spiritual inheritance. 1:14

❑ Our life is found in Jesus. 2:5

❑ Authority in the heavenlies is ours in Christ. 2:6

❑ We have been saved. 2:8

❑ God is the master craftsman of our lives. 2:10

❑ We are created for good works. 2:10

❑ Jesus' blood purchased a close relationship with Father God. 2:13

❑ We have peace. 2:14, 15

❑ There is nothing separating us from God. 2:16

❑ Access to the Father's throne at any time is ours. 2:18; 3:12

❑ We are citizens of heaven. 2:19

❑ We are members of God's household. 2:19

❑ The word of God is our foundation for everything. 2:20

❑ God has made his home within us. 2:22

❑ We can understand God's will for us. 3:4-6

❑ All nations have been reconciled to God. 3:6

❑ There is one body of Christ and we are members. 3:6

❑ The promises of Jesus are for us all. 3:6

❑ You and I can reveal God's wisdom. 3:10

❑ God's love becomes our solid foundation. 3:17

This is not intended to be an all-inclusive list, but it should stir our minds to realize that we really need to grasp who we are in Christ. We are not just filling time until our deaths; we are the children of God, royalty, with a divine purpose. As we begin to realize who we are, then we realize

> **"Many believers have stumbled through their Christian walk simply because they did not realize who they were in Christ."**

the authority, power and dominion we truly possess. Many believers have stumbled through their Christian walk simply because they did not realize who they were in Christ.

Paul, in writing to the church at Rome, gave us some insight into our destiny in Christ. Referring to those who were born again, he stated that we were destined to be like Jesus!

> For **whom he did foreknow, he also did predestinate to be conformed to the image of his Son,** that he might be the firstborn among many brethren.
>
> Romans 8:29

If we were predestined to be like Jesus, then I want to know what he was like.

As an ex-military man, I understand that I had to first learn about the capabilities of the armed service I was in, my job description, and who I was before I would ever be able to combat an enemy. Why is it that the church insists on knowing all about the capabilities of Satan (which are usually reports the enemy has given, otherwise known as propagandized misinformation) rather than what our commander and chief has said? God takes great measures to tell us about us first, and then the devil's true abilities (known as proper intelligence reports)! My contention is that we first recognize who we are before we try to learn about the devices of our enemy. The writer of Hebrews gives us a detailed account of what the Lord Jesus is like.

> **He (Jesus) is the sole expression of the glory of God—[the Light-being, the out-raying of the divine]—and He is the perfect imprint *and* very image of [God's] nature, upholding *and* maintaining *and* guiding *and* propelling the universe by His mighty word of power.** When He had *by offering Himself* accomplished *our* cleansing of sins *and* riddance of guilt, He sat down at the right hand of the divine Majesty on high, [taking a place and rank by which] He Himself became as much superior to the angels as the glorious Name (title) which He has inherited is different from *and* more excellent than theirs.
>
> Hebrews 1:3a-4(AMP)

You and I have the privilege of being just like Jesus. Ephesians chapter two says that we are seated in heavenly places in Christ Jesus. As we begin to realize who we are, we will begin to operate effectively in true "spiritual warfare."

Notice, the writer of Hebrews gave us a biblical definition of the nature of Jesus. He is the "sole expression of the glory of God." If I am predestinated to be like Him, then I should be an expression of God's glory. Jesus prayed that I would be one with Him just as He was one with the Father

(John 17:11, 21). If I am one with Him, then I should be identical in expression (out-raying of the divine nature). Jesus is the "perfect imprint" of God. When people look at you and I, do they see a perfect imprint of our heavenly Father? Do they see the very image of God's nature? If not, what are we doing trying to wrestle with devils?

The Holy Spirit gave us a powerful understanding of how Jesus operates. He upholds, guides, maintains, and propels the universe by His mighty word of power. We should key in on this. If our world is spinning wildly out of control (not just our world universal, but *OUR* world: daily lives, jobs, families, activities, ministry, etc.), it then becomes evident that we are not operating in the word of God. No matter what circumstance comes our way, we are well able to deal with every situation according to God's directives. Just like Jesus, we need to uphold, guide, maintain, and propel our universe by His mighty word of power.

Upholding Our World

Everything in our daily lives should begin with the word. To uphold means to maintain or support morally or spiritually. Our support for all that we do comes from God's word. The only way you and I can uphold our world is by His word. I am convinced that everything we face daily can be dealt with according to the word of God. Paul wrote to the church at Corinth to encourage them with the trials they were going through.

> *There hath no temptation taken you but such as is common to man: but God is faithful, who will not suffer you to be temped above that ye are able; but will with the temptation also make a way to escape, that ye may be able to bear it.*
>
> *1 Corinthians 10:13*

James said to "count it all joy" when we face various trials because the trying of our faith works patience (James 1:2). We could say it like this: "the trying of the word in us builds patience." Another way to say it would be, "the trying of the word in us *works patience*." Or even, "without the word in us (faith), patience alone doesn't work."

> **"As we allow the word of God a place of primacy in our lives, we position ourselves for the fulfillment of our destiny."**

Jesus, in Luke chapter 8 verse 15 stated that fruit is produced by patience. As we allow the word of God a place of primacy in our lives, we position ourselves for the fulfillment of our destiny. Without a basis in the word, we predetermine our actions will be separate from the will of God. God's word is the alpha and omega, the starting point and ending point for all we will do. If we are to uphold our world, we must allow the word of God preeminence in our lives!

Maintaining Our World

Like Jesus, we are to maintain our world. The word "maintain" means: (1) to keep or keep up; carry on, (2) to keep in continuance or in a certain state, as of repair. When I think of maintenance, I often think of the routine things in life that must be done. Irresponsible people often wait for things to break before paying attention to them. Whether it is an automobile, appliance, or even their marriages, they wait for the problem to manifest before making it a priority.

When I was in the United States Navy, we performed routine checks known as preventive maintenance. The objective was to take care of items *before* they broke down. Regular maintenance insures years of operation.

Within the church, we so often vacillate. One day we are up, the next we are down—driven by our circumstances and every wind of doctrine that comes along. We wait for something to go wrong in our lives and then we try to fix it. A daily dosage of preventive maintenance in the word would do so much to prevent our future breakdowns. Why do we wait for marriage problems to arise before we find out God's plan for successful marriages? Why do we wait for our children to run away before we seek godly counsel for raising children? Why do we wait for a diagnosis of a fatal disease before we try to discover what God has said concerning our health? If we are to maintain our world by the word of God, then we must have a regular diet of the word in our lives.

Guiding Our World

This area is a daily decision to allow the Holy Spirit to direct our steps according to the word of God. The word "guide" means: to point out the way for; lead. Many of us only look for the wisdom of God when the situation seems too difficult for us to handle. We need to guide our world by the word of God daily. If we will, we will not feel so awkward and uncomfortable when we are in his presence. Through the word of God we will be successful in all our endeavors.

Thy word is a lamp unto my feet, and a light unto my path.
Psalm 119:105

Trust in the LORD *with all thine heart; and lean not unto thine own understanding.*

Proverbs 3:5

If the direction of our life is not going the way we want it to, I would submit that we have not allowed the word of God to guide our lives. God is willing to show us every step of the way if we will become receptive to His word and voice.

Propelling Our World

I see this area as one of advancement. The word "propel" means: to drive forward. The word of God literally needs to be the catalyst behind every decision we make. When others look at our lives they should see the hand of God all over us. There should be no question that our lives are being thrust into destiny according to the word of God.

The Apostle Paul's letter to the church at Ephesus details many things concerning our legal positioning in Christ. Before we try to fight the devils of Ephesians six, let us understand this positioning in the first three chapters. I do not believe that those who do not yet know who they are in Christ should be trying to enter into demonic warfare. That is not to say that the new believer does not have authority. They do! It simply means that before we fly the airplane, let's learn to drive the car. Before we drive the car, let's learn to ride the bike. Before we ride the bike, let's learn to ride the trike. Before we ride the trike, let's learn to run. Before we run, let's learn to walk. Before we walk, let's learn to stand. Before we stand, let's learn to crawl. There is nothing wrong with any of these stages, however we must recognize our level and be content to grow from there rather than deceiving ourselves into believing we are at a level we are still trying to achieve. Many believers are legends in their own minds. I believe in walking by faith and receiving by faith, but not deceiving ourselves by foolishness disguised as faith.

Before you and I enter into battle, let us first complete boot camp, progress on to our specialized training, become assigned to a local unit (church), submit to the authorities in that local unit (five-fold ministry under the direction of the local Pastor), and allow them to direct us into proper positioning and thereby effectively enter true spiritual warfare. (For some, simple submission to God's local authority will be the only warfare they can handle!) Let us accomplish this, not with our personalized agendas, but listening for, receiving and bringing to completion the assignments given by our local commanders.

Keys to Remember

Who Am I?

❏ You are a child of God, royalty, with a divine purpose.

❏ Recognize who you are in Christ before you learn about the devices of our enemy.

❏ A daily dosage of preventive maintenance in the word would do so much to prevent future breakdowns.

❏ Make a daily decision to allow the Holy Spirit to direct your steps according to the word of God.

❏ As believers, we should first complete boot camp, progress on to our specialized training, become assigned to a local unit (church), submit to the authorities in that local unit (five-fold ministry under the direction of the local Pastor), and allow them to direct us into proper positioning and thereby effectively enter true spiritual warfare.

CHAPTER SIX

Walking Like Jesus

Walk worthy! As I mentioned in the last chapter, I am firmly convinced that we must recognize who we are in Christ before we will ever be effective in true spiritual warfare (the ability to appropriate and enact the word of God in any given situation or circumstance). You and I are commanded to walk worthy of the vocation—calling and destiny —that is upon our lives. The call of God is God's assignment in your life. It is His divine will and purpose for you. I am firmly convinced that an individual's purpose in God cannot be fully realized separated from the local church. **IT IS GOD'S WILL** that you are a responsible and productive member in a local church.

When I joined the United States Navy, I became a part of the United States Navy universal. This is what happens when one is born again. They become a part of the body of Christ universal. When I enlisted, even though I was a part of the Navy universal, I was not effective or usable to the Navy until I was thoroughly trained and then assigned to a local unit. So it is within the body of Christ. Even though we are a part of the body universal, we are not effective or usable until we are assigned in a local church. Notice what follows God's command to walk worthy of the vocation— calling and destiny—He has placed in your life.

The Apostle Paul states that we are to "walk worthy of the vocation wherewith ye are called, *with all lowliness and meekness, with longsuffering, forbearing one anoth-*

er in love; endeavoring to keep the unity of the Spirit in the bond of peace." How do you do this by yourself? I have heard many say, "Pastor, I don't need to be in a local church to love God." Yes you do. Here is what God says about the subject of loving Him:

> **And this is love, that we walk after his commandments.** *This is the commandment, That, as ye have heard from the beginning, ye should walk in it.*
>
> *2 John 1:6*

Since God's word is true, we must obey His commands if we are going to love Him. What are His commands concerning the local church and proper submission? Paul wrote to the Ephesian church and said we must walk worthy with all longsuffering, forbearing **one another in love.** You cannot accomplish this by yourself separated from the local church. He also said, "endeavoring to keep the **unity** of the spirit." Again, you cannot accomplish this isolated from the body of Christ. If you wrestle with loving yourself or personal disunity, with no one else around, **you need deliverance . . .** or a therapist! What else does the Lord command?

> **Not forsaking the assembling of ourselves together,** *as the manner of some is; but exhorting one another: and so much the more, as ye see the day approaching.*
>
> *Hebrews 10:25*

> **Obey them that have the rule over you, and submit yourselves:** *for they watch for your souls, as they that*

must give account, that they may do it with joy, and not with grief: for that is unprofitable for you.

Hebrews 13:17

God commands us to not forsake the gathering together of ourselves. We need to be with each other in order to fulfill the commands of God and His destiny for our lives. How do we obey those over us if we are not in a local church where there is God-ordained authority in our lives?

> *For the time is come that **judgment must begin at the house of God:** and if it first begin at us, what shall the end be of them that obey not the gospel of God?*
>
> *1 Peter 4:17*

I love this passage of scripture because it states that judgment begins at the house of God, the local church. Then it refers to those outside the church as those who do not obey the gospel of God. We already have read that if we love God, we obey Him. Therefore true obedience begins at the house of God or the local church! If we truly love God, we will be in His house, submitted to His authority. God placed the five-fold ministry within the local church to cause us to mature, thereby perfecting our love for Him.

> *And hereby we do know that we know him, if we keep his commandments. He that saith, I know him, and keepeth not his commandments, is a liar, and the truth is not in him. **But whoso keepeth his word, in him verily is the love of God perfected:** hereby know we that we are in him.*
>
> *1 John 2:3-5*

*By this we know that we love the children of God, when we love God, and keep his commandments. For **this is the love of God, that we keep his commandments:** and his commandments are not grievous.*

1 John 5:2-3

God doesn't want us simply enlisting in the body of Christ, He wants us to walk worthy in the body of Christ. If one can walk worthy, one can also walk unworthy. We need to be a new breed that wants to honor God with our entire being. We must have a burning desire to become a vital part within the body. In proper context, the responsibilities of Ephesians chapters four through six, deal with our part in the body of Christ enacted through proper submission and obedience within the local church.

> **"True obedience begins at the house of God, the local church!"**

Now within the context of the local church, let us take a brief look at the last few chapters in the book of Ephesians. These chapters deal with our responsibilities in the Lord. Let me highlight some of them.

❑ Live a life that reflects Jesus. 4:1
❑ Be humble and gentle. 4:2
❑ Be patient. 4:2
❑ Always let love determine your actions. 4:2
❑ Strive for unity. 4:3
❑ Recognize the grace and gifts given to us. 4:7-11

❑ Accept God's authority structure. 4:11-12
❑ Grow up and mature in God. 4:13-16
❑ Always speak the truth in love. 4:15
❑ Don't live like the world (doing what everyone else does). 4:17-19
❑ Eliminate bad behaviors in your life. 4:20-22
❑ Change the way you think and act. Follow the Bible in your daily habits. 4:23-24
❑ Quit lying. 4:25
❑ When angry, don't give way to sin. 4:26
❑ The devil doesn't deserve anything that belongs to you. 4:27
❑ Watch what you say. Guard your speech. 4:28
❑ Always do what is pleasing to God. 4:30
❑ Eliminate all bitterness, rage and anger. 4:31
❑ Be kind and compassionate to one another. 4:32
❑ Forgive each other quickly, just like God forgave you. 4:32
❑ Imitate God's characteristics and qualities. 5:1
❑ Live a life of love. 5:2
❑ Eliminate sexual immorality and greed. 5:3
❑ Stop using obscene language and telling rude jokes. 5:4
❑ Know the truth and avoid deceptions. 5:6
❑ Walk away from those who want to sin. 5:7
❑ Live like a child of God. 5:8
❑ Find out what pleases the Lord. 5:10
❑ Eliminate and expose fruitless deeds of darkness. 5:11-14
❑ Walk in the wisdom of the Bible, not in your own rationale. 5:15
❑ Make the most of every opportunity. 5:16
❑ Find out God's plan for your life. 5:17

- ❑ Do not get drunk. 5:18
- ❑ Be filled with the Spirit of God. 5:18
- ❑ Always have a song of encouragement in your heart. 5:19
- ❑ Give thanks to God for everything. 5:20
- ❑ Submit to one another out of reverence for Christ. 5:21
- ❑ Wives, submit to your husbands. 5:22-24
- ❑ Husbands, love your wives. 5:25-33
- ❑ Children, obey your parents. 6:1
- ❑ Honor your father and mother. 6:2, 3
- ❑ Fathers, train and instruct your children in the things of God. 6:4
- ❑ Obey those in authority over you. 6:5-8
- ❑ Treat kindly those who work for you. 6:9

Finally

- ❑ Find your strength in the Lord. 6:10
- ❑ Put on the full armor of God. 6:11, 13-17
- ❑ Recognize your true struggle. 6:12
- ❑ Pray for the men of God. 6:19

> **"I personally believe that when we appropriate the provisions of the cross, God is ecstatic! That is true spiritual warfare."**

We could spend a great deal of time dealing with each one of these. The point of this book, however, is not to give a full revelation or discourse on the book of Ephesians, but to motivate us to search the scripture for ourselves so that we are fully equipped for every good work in the Lord. Again, this is not intended to be an all-inclusive list but a highlight of what we often miss when we talk about spiritual warfare. We all rush to get to the struggle! It should not be that way.

The first thing we must do after we have developed ourselves in the Lord (Chapters 1-3 of Ephesians) is to find out our place in the body of Christ. Paul instructed the church in Corinth that many people had died because they did not realize and properly discern their placement in the body.

> *For he that eateth and drinketh unworthily, eateth and drinketh damnation to himself, not discerning the Lord's body.* **For this cause many are weak and sickly among you, and many sleep.**
>
> *1 Corinthians 11:29-30*

How many people come to church week after week eating and drinking unworthily because they are walking unworthily? Is it any wonder that people remain sick, in poverty, lacking dominion and never overcoming anything? True warfare isn't blaming the devil for that state, but recognizing that we have not appropriated and enacted the word of God in our situation and then making the proper changes. Second, we must get along with our brothers and sisters in the Lord. Too many in the church are fighting with one another. You cannot be effective fighting devils when you are caught up like Satan as an accuser of the brethren. Third, we must recognize and accept God's leaders in our lives as gifts and submit to their authority. Fourth, we must be renewing our minds and simply act like God. He is the one who enables us to operate in the fruit and gifts of His spirit. Live a life of love and forgiveness. Fifth, we must eliminate the ways of the world that have become so customary in our lives—sexual immorality, impurities, greed, obscenity, foolish talk and coarse joking. We cannot afford to be a partner with the works of darkness. How can we fight the good fight of faith when we have yielded to the works of the flesh? Sixth, let us find out what pleases God. We know that faith pleases Him (Hebrews 11:6). I personally believe that when we appropriate the provisions of the cross, God is ecstatic! That is true spiritual warfare. Be in submission to one another and those in authority. This pleases the Father. Seventh, have a great family life. Eighth, be faithful with your employer or employees, whichever the case may be. Honor the Lord in everything that you do for the kingdom of God. When all of these things are in order, we can gain some understanding into the *"finally"* Paul was talking about.

When we truly understand the book of Ephesians, we can see the Apostle Paul was not speaking about fighting devils as much as he was instructing us on how we should be conducting our own lives.

Keys to Remember

Walking Like Jesus

❑   Walk worthy of God's call in your life.

❑   Find out your place in the body of Christ.

❑   We must get along with our brothers and sisters in the Lord.

❑   Recognize and accept God's leaders in your life as gifts and submit to their authority.

❑   Renew your mind and simply act like God.

❑   Eliminate the ways of the world that may have become customary in your life.

❑   Realize that faith is what pleases God. Walk in the word.

❑   Have a great family life.

❑   Be faithful with your employer or employees.

CHAPTER SEVEN

The Armor of God

Medieval times have always fascinated me. Stories of knights in suits of armor and their harrowing tales of victory. On a recent trip to the United Kingdom my curiosity and imagination were both sparked as I visited several castles. Many of them contained beautiful pieces of art, antiques, relics and marvelous architecture. But what really caught my attention were the various suits of armor. No two suits were the same. Even though they served the same purpose, they were never alike because they were made specifically for their owner.

In Ephesians chapter six we find another type of armor. This is the armor of God that is available to all of us who have made Jesus Christ the Lord of our lives. But like the armor of old, this armor is suited to its owner. The more knowledge you possess about the word of God, the more effective you will be in life. Your ability to stand against the treachery of the devil is dependent upon your knowledge of the word of God. Every piece of this armor is derived from His word. The way we are going to defeat the devil is by appropriating and enacting the word of God in every situation and circumstance we face. This does not mean that we start rebuking Satan for everything that happens in our lives. No, we submit to God, resist the devil and he flees.

Submit yourselves therefore to God. Resist the devil, and he will flee from you.

James 4:7

The church has thought that trying to stand in our own abilities, our own will-power, our own determination was resisting the devil. Not at all! It is in our ability to submit to God, His structure and authority. The devil flees not because of our great stand of self-denial or abasement, but because of our positioning in submission to God.

> **"The devil flees not because of our great stand of self-denial or abasement, but because of our positioning in submission to God."**

When we realize this, we are now on our way to being extremely effective in true spiritual warfare. Even the armor the Apostle Paul lists in Ephesians chapter six is derived from the word of God and not in our knowledge of or resistance to the devil.

(1) ". . . having your loins girt about with truth . . ."

Sanctify them through thy truth: **thy word is truth.**
John 17:17

(2) ". . . having on the breastplate of righteousness . . ."

My tongue shall speak of **thy word: for all thy commandments are righteousness.**

Psalm 119:172

All the words of my mouth are in righteousness;

Proverbs 8:8a

I have sworn by myself, **the word is gone out of my mouth in righteousness,**

Isaiah 45:23a

By the **word of truth,** *by the power of God, by the* **armour of righteousness,**

2 Corinthians 6:7a

(3) ". . . feet shod with the preparation of the gospel of peace . . ."

In whom ye also trusted, after that ye heard **the word of truth, the gospel** *of your salvation . . .*

Ephesians 1:13a

For the hope which is laid up for you in heaven, whereof ye heard before in **the word of the truth of the gospel;**

Colossians 1:5

But the word of the Lord endureth for ever. And this is **the word which by the gospel** *is preached unto you.*

1 Peter 1:25

(4) ". . . taking the shield of faith . . ."

But what saith it? The **word is nigh thee,** *even in thy mouth, and in thy heart: that is,* **the word of faith,** *which we preach;*

Romans 10:8

So then faith cometh by hearing, and hearing by the word of God.

Romans 10:17

If thou put the brethren in remembrance of these things, thou shalt be a good minister of Jesus Christ, **nourished up in the words of faith** *and of good doctrine, whereunto thou hast attained.*

1 Timothy 4:6

(5) ". . . take the helmet of salvation . . ."

Let thy mercies come also unto me, O LORD, even thy **salvation, according to thy word.**

Psalm 119:41

Men and brethren, children of the stock of Abraham, and whosoever among you feareth God, to you is the **word of this salvation** *sent.*

Acts 13:26

In whom ye also trusted, after that ye heard the **word of truth, the gospel of your salvation:** *in whom also after that ye believed, ye were sealed with that holy Spirit of promise,*

Ephesians 1:13

(6) ". . . take the sword of the Spirit . . ."

> *And take . . .* **the sword of the Spirit, which is the word of God:**
>
> Ephesians 6:17

> *For the* **word of God is quick, and powerful, and sharper than any two edged sword . . .**
>
> Hebrews 4:12a

> *And he had in his right hand seven stars: and* **out of his mouth went a sharp two edged sword:** *and his countenance was as the sun shineth in his strength.*
>
> Revelation 1:16

This armor originally was given to Jesus. He in turn gave it to us.

> *Yea, truth faileth; and he that departeth from evil maketh himself a prey: and* **the LORD saw it,** *and it displeased him that there was no judgment. And he saw that there was no man, and wondered that there was no intercessor: therefore* **his arm brought salvation unto him;** *and his righteousness, it sustained him.* **For he put on righteousness as a breastplate, and an helmet of salvation upon his head; and he put on the garments of vengeance for clothing, and was clad with zeal as a cloke.** *According to their deeds, accordingly he will repay, fury to his adversaries, recompence to his enemies; to the islands he will repay recompence. So shall they fear the name of the LORD from the west, and his glory from the rising of the sun.* **When the enemy shall come in like**

a flood, the Spirit of the LORD shall lift up a standard against him.

Isaiah 59:15-19

We often quote the last part of this passage. *"When the enemy shall come in like a flood, the Spirit of the LORD shall lift up a standard against him."* What is this really talking about? The passage begins by saying, "truth faileth." This simply means that the people were no longer standing for truth. We have already learned that truth is based solely upon the word of God. The armor that was given to us—the same armor given to Jesus—was given to raise a standard of the word against the deception and onslaught of the enemy.

As you can see, every piece of the armor is derived from God's word. This is why true spiritual warfare is the ability to appropriate and enact the word of God in any given situation or circumstance. If we are to fight this good fight of faith, we must be willing to properly discern true "spiritual warfare," then face and defeat the ultimate enemy.

Keys to Remember

The Armor of God

❑ The way we are going to defeat the devil is by appropriating and enacting the word of God in every situation and circumstance we face.

❑ The armor that was given to us—the same armor given to Jesus—was given to raise a standard of the word against the deception and onslaught of the enemy.

❑ Every piece of the armor is derived from God's word.

CHAPTER EIGHT

Demonic Warfare

The demonic aspect of spiritual warfare is one that I will cover more extensively in another book. However, I would like to show this particular aspect to give us a better understanding of who we are in Christ and our positioning in Him. God gives us a little window through the prophet Isaiah to enable us to see more clearly the deception of personal exaltation against the word of God. True spiritual warfare (the ability to appropriate and enact the word of God in any given situation or circumstance) begins in the mind with choices we make to follow the word of God. Satan himself allowed selfish thoughts of ambition to lead him to his downfall.

> *How art thou fallen from heaven, O Lucifer, son of the morning! how art thou cut down to the ground, which didst weaken the nations!* **For thou hast said in thine heart, I will ascend into heaven, I will exalt my throne above the stars of God: I will sit also upon the mount of the congregation, in the sides of the north: I will ascend above the heights of the clouds; I will be like the most High.**
>
> *Isaiah 14:12-14*

The above scripture from the book of Isaiah details Satan's error. We have heard for years that Satan fell because of pride. This is true but there is so much more to be said about his fall. Notice, his pride was not something that was outwardly manifested, but something he said in his heart! God judged the intent of his heart.

> *For the word of God is living and active. Sharper than any double-edged sword, it penetrates even to dividing soul and spirit, joints and marrow;* **it judges the thoughts and attitudes of the heart.**
>
> *Hebrews 4:12 (NIV)*

Many people today believe that sin is not sin until it is acted upon. God has a different perspective. Remember what Jesus said when simply talking about the area of adultery.

> *But I say unto you, That* **whosoever looketh** *on a woman* **to lust** *after her* **hath committed adultery with her already in his heart.**
>
> *Matthew 5:28*

I could paraphrase what Jesus said like this: "a look of lust begins the conception of sin within the heart." James carried this explanation even further so we could not mistake the meaning. He describes lust (a strong desire) as the beginning of sin.

> *Let no man say when he is tempted, I am tempted of God: for God cannot be tempted with evil, neither tempteth he any man:* **But every man is tempted, when he is drawn away of his own lust,** *and enticed.* **Then when lust hath conceived, it bringeth forth sin:** *and sin, when it is finished, bringeth forth death.*
>
> *James 1:13-15*

Sin does not begin when we commit an act. Sin begins the moment we entertain the seeds of lust that are contrary to the word of God with an intent to carry them out. The devil isn't even the one tempting us. It is our own strong desire that leads us astray. It is only after those weaknesses in our lives are revealed that the demonic realm can **entice** us with further temptation. Satan is not all-knowing and does not know our weaknesses until we display them. His major weapon is preying upon our weaknesses. That is why Peter said the devil is *"seeking whom he may devour"* (1 Peter 5:8). He is looking for our weaknesses.

> **"Satan is not all-knowing and does not know our weaknesses until we display them."**

Satan's fall was because of his lusts that were revealed by his selfish and prideful thoughts. His intent was to carry them out and as a result, God judged him. We know that the fall of Satan was prior to the creation of man in Genesis chapter one because he was already present to tempt man. As I was meditating on this passage of scripture, the Holy Spirit revealed something to me. When God judged Satan for his prideful statements, he then created man to have all of the qualities Satan desired. Let me show them to you from a scriptural standpoint. Let me show you Satan's five declarations as revealed by the prophet Isaiah, and then show you our positioning according to the word of God.

(1) I will ascend into heaven

It is interesting to me that the devil made this declaration. This is a statement of relationship. It is a statement of desiring to be one with God. This type of relationship was something he did not possess. The Apostle Paul gave us some insight into this statement when he was instructing the church at Rome concerning faith.

> *But the righteousness which is of faith speaketh on this wise, Say not in thine heart, Who shall ascend into heaven? (that is, to bring Christ down from above:)*
>
> *Romans 10:6*

Because of our relationship with God, we never have to say, "I will ascend into heaven," because God is in us. Satan did not have that type of relationship with God and desired it. He would never be on the same plane as God. Jesus prayed that you and I would be one with God.

> **That they all may be one;** *as thou, Father, art in me, and I in thee,* **that they also may be one in us:** *that the world may believe that thou hast sent me.*
>
> *John 17:21*

When you and I are born again, we are seated in heavenly places in Christ Jesus!

> **But God,** *who is rich in mercy, for his great love wherewith he loved us, Even when we were dead in sins,* **hath quickened us together with Christ,** *(by grace ye are saved;)*

And hath raised us up together, **and made us sit together in heavenly places in Christ Jesus:**

Ephesians 2:4-6

We don't need to bring God down to our level (which
is how many people interpret their relationship with God, on
their level!) because we have been elevated to His level in
Christ Jesus. When the devil looks at us, his jealousy burns
because we have the relationship with God he desired.

(2) I will exalt my throne above the stars of God

What exactly was the devil trying to say? First he
wants to elevate his throne (position of authority) over the
stars of God. This is not a natural star such as a sun, but
another being that possessed a level of authority. I would
submit that the stars of God are the angels of God or God's
messengers. Here is what is recorded in the book of Job.

When the **morning stars sang together,** *and all the sons
of God shouted for joy?*

Job 38:7

These stars (angels) sang together. They were present before
the foundation of the world. According to the story of creation, the natural stars were not created until after the creation of the world. These stars sang, however, at the creation
of the world. Notice what the Apostle John states in his revelation of Jesus.

*The mystery of the seven stars which thou sawest in my right
hand, and the seven golden candlesticks. The* **seven stars are**

the angels of the seven churches: and the seven candlesticks which thou sawest are the seven churches.

Revelation 1:20

This passage clearly shows that the seven stars are angels or messengers to the seven churches. Whether they are local pastors or angelic beings, they are not physical stars like our sun.

And the fifth angel sounded, and I saw a star fall from heaven unto the earth: and to him was given the key of the bottomless pit.

Revelation 9:1

John continues and sees a star fall from heaven, and unto **him,** was given the key to the bottomless pit. Again this is not a natural star but an angelic being. Why would he have to exalt his throne above the angels? Interesting question, but suffice it to say he was looking for a position of authority that he did not possess.

On the other hand, you and I will sit in judgment over angels! We were created to have and exercise the authority Satan only aspired to possess.

Know ye not that we shall judge angels? *how much more things that pertain to this life?*

1 Corinthians 6:3

(3) I will sit also upon the mount of the congregation

Not only did he want to exalt his throne, but he wanted to exercise authority from that exalted position. This was not a position that had been given to the devil. This was a position he would never hold. Any authority he operates in today has been given to him by those who are blatantly disobedient to the voice of God or ignorant of his devices and their own authority.

Jesus gave us all authority and the right to act upon the authority we have as the children of God. We not only have the right to operate like Jesus, but a mandate. Through the name of Jesus we eliminate the operations of the demonic realm. No wonder Satan hates a believer who understands their positioning in Christ.

> *Behold,* ***I give unto you power (authority)*** *to tread on serpents and scorpions, and* **over all the power of the enemy:** *and nothing shall by any means hurt you.*
>
> *Luke 10:19*

> ***And these signs shall follow them that believe; In my name shall they cast out devils;*** *they shall speak with new tongues; They shall take up serpents; and if they drink any deadly thing, it shall not hurt them; they shall lay hands on the sick, and they shall recover.*
>
> *Mark 16:17-18*

You and I have been given the right to exercise authority. Not only over the devil and his minions, but over our own lives. The Greek word for authority is, *exousia.* It literally means authority but carries the meaning of unlimited possibilities and the right to act on those possibilities. You and I are not limited to the abilities of this natural realm. We have the abilities of a supernatural realm that our Father has given us the right to operate in. This is the position Satan desired to have.

(4) I will ascend above the heights of the clouds

Satan wanted the authority, the right to act on that authority, and the limitless possibilities that accompanied such authority. He did not want to be bound to the limitations of this world. He desired to be above the darkness that this world was in (Genesis 1:2). God created man to have this authority and to not be bound by the conditions of this world. God ordained man to change these conditions and cause them to line up to the purposes of God. You and I are not of this world. Just like Jesus, we are born of God, in the world with all authority, and returning to God. We may be in this world for a time, but we are not of the world.

> *Jesus knowing that the Father had given all things into his hands, and that he was come from God, and went to God;*
>
> *John 13:3*

> *If ye were of the world, the world would love his own: but because* ***ye are not of the world, but I have chosen you out of the world,*** *therefore the world hateth you.*
>
> *John 15:19*

> *I have given them thy word; and the world hath hated them,* ***because they are not of the world, even as I am not of the world.*** *I pray not that thou shouldest take them out of the world, but that thou shouldest keep them from the*

evil. **They are not of the world, even as I am not of the world.**

John 17:14-16

(5) I will be like the Most High

The ultimate statement Satan made was one that said he would be like God himself. Remember, God called all of these statements of pride sinful. Whether people like it or not, *you and I* were created to be just like God. We are God's representatives in the planet earth and we are just like him.

> *And* **God said, Let us make man in our image, after our likeness:** *and let them have dominion over the fish of the sea, and over the fowl of the air, and over the cattle, and over all the earth, and over every creeping thing that creepeth upon the earth. So* **God created man in his own image, in the image of God created he him; male and female created he them.** *And God blessed them, and God said unto them, Be fruitful, and multiply, and replenish the earth, and subdue it: and have dominion over the fish of the sea, and over the fowl of the air, and over every living thing that moveth upon the earth.*

Genesis 1:26-28

> *Herein is our love made perfect, that we may have boldness in the day of judgment:* **because as he is, so are we in this world.**

1 John 4:17

When we truly realize who we are in Christ, the devil becomes so insignificant. My desire is to expose Satan's lies of supremacy, which he has propagated in the world, which began in his heart long before man was created. I pray that we would hear the words of Jesus!

And he said unto them, **I beheld Satan as lightning fall** *from heaven.*

Luke 10:18

> **"When we truly realize who we are in Christ, the devil becomes so insignificant."**

The devil is a defeated foe. No wonder he hates us so. We represent everything he aspired to be. Let us not give up our authority to one who has already been defeated. Let us realize that the devil is not our problem. If he is not our problem, then why are there so many Christians living defeated lives?

Keys to Remember

Demonic Warfare

☐ True spiritual warfare (the ability to appropriate and enact the word of God in any given situation or circumstance) begins in the mind with choices we make to follow the word of God.

☐ Satan himself allowed selfish thoughts of ambition to lead him to his downfall.

☐ Satan's pride was not something that was outwardly manifested, but something he said in his heart! God judged the intent of his heart.

☐ Sin begins the moment we entertain the seeds of lust that are contrary to the word of God with an intent to carry them out.

☐ The devil is a defeated foe. We represent everything he aspired to be.

CHAPTER NINE

The Ultimate Enemy

As we have seen, spiritual warfare is not a new concept to mankind. From the beginning of Genesis we can see the conflict in which man has been involved. God created man to have authority, power and dominion in the planet earth. Satan's desire was to exalt himself above God. When that act of rebellion resulted in a forceful departure from heaven, he set his sights upon achieving authority wherever possible. Since Satan could not take God's position, he set his eyes on the authority of man.

> *And God said, Let us make man in our image, after our likeness: and let them have dominion over the fish of the sea, and over the fowl of the air, and over the cattle, and over all the earth, and over every creeping thing that creepeth upon the earth. So God created man in his own image, in the image of God created he him; male and female created he them. And God blessed them, and God said unto them, Be fruitful, and multiply, and replenish the earth, and subdue it: and have dominion over the fish of the sea, and over the fowl of the air, and over every living thing that moveth upon the earth.*
>
> *Genesis 1:26-28*

Man was given complete authority in the earth. That included all authority over the devil and his operations. Man did not have to wrestle with the devil for authority, *he had been given authority by God!* All he had to do was stand upon the declarations of God and Satan would never gain any foothold over man upon this planet. In Genesis chapter two, we see more of the word of the Lord that came to Adam.

> *And the LORD God commanded the man, saying, Of every tree of the garden thou mayest freely eat: But of the tree of the knowledge of good and evil, thou shalt not eat of it: for in the day that thou eatest thereof thou shalt surely die.*
>
> *Genesis 2:16-17*

God instructed Adam how to operate successfully in this new environment in which he had been placed. God had made him to be the guardian of this world. Everything was at his disposal. God placed only one requirement upon Adam. He was to care for all within the garden, but the tree in the middle belonged to God. Adam was allowed to be the

> **"The devil's only intent is to steal, kill, and destroy."**

steward of the tree, but he could not partake of it. (Sounds like the first tithe, doesn't it?)

In Genesis chapter three, Satan comes to challenge this authority. His desire was to be the god of this world (2 Corinthians 4:4), a title Adam possessed. He came deceiving Eve pretending to be a messenger that would bring a truth God had hidden from her. Adam knew better but abdicated his authority by standing idle while Satan was attempting to deceive his wife. Remember, the devil's only intent was to steal, kill, and destroy (John 10:10). His mode of operation is the same today. He will not even show up unless he intends to accomplish one of those three things. He may promise the world, but *his only intent is to steal, kill and destroy!*

> *Now the serpent was more subtil than any beast of the field which the LORD God had made. And he said unto the woman, Yea, hath God said, Ye shall not eat of every tree of the garden? And the woman said unto the serpent, We may eat of the fruit of the trees of the garden: But of the fruit of the tree which is in the midst of the garden, God hath said, Ye shall not eat of it, neither shall ye touch it, lest ye die. And the serpent said unto the woman, Ye shall not surely die: For God doth know that in the day ye eat thereof, then your eyes shall be opened, and ye shall be as gods, knowing good and evil. And when the woman saw that the tree was good for food, and that it was pleasant to the eyes, and a tree to be desired to make one wise, she took of the fruit thereof, and did eat, and gave also unto her husband with her; and he did eat.*
>
> Genesis 3:1-6

God records the fall of man so we could clearly see how the enemy operates with blatant lies intended to deceive. The devil doesn't use anything new. There is nothing new under the sun (Ecclesiastes 1:9b).

First, the enemy asked Eve if she knew what God said. When she appeared to have some knowledge, he then questioned her understanding of the word. Next he denied the word spoken and finally put his deceptive twist upon it. The enemy still works the same way today. He is seeking whom he may devour (1 Peter 5:7). He looks to see if we have any knowledge, then questions our understanding.

Next, he will try to get us to question the validity of the word. Last, if we won't deny the word, he will put a deceptive twist upon it so we have the wrong meaning. The Apostle John records how man can still fall to the deception of the enemy.

> *For all that is in the world,* **the lust of the flesh, and the lust of the eyes, and the pride of life,** *is not of the Father, but is of the world.*
>
> *1 John 2:16*

Please notice, Satan cannot blatantly steal, kill or destroy anything where he has not been given a legal right by man. We are our own worst enemy. Everything John mentions comes from the heart of man and not from the devil. He simply capitalizes upon our sin towards, or ignorance of God's word. Take a look again at a comparison of the Apostle John's words and Genesis chapter three.

(1) ". . . the lust of the flesh . . ."

> *. . . when the woman saw that the tree was good for food . . .*

(2) ". . . the lust of the eyes . . ."

> *. . . that it was pleasant to the eyes . . .*

(3) ". . . the pride of life . . ."

> *. . . and a tree to be desired to make one wise . . .*

Eve fell to the lust of the flesh, lust of the eyes and the pride of life. Satan was only a catalyst to get her to take a closer look at each one.

I do not believe that Eve would have been deceived had she had firsthand knowledge of what the Lord had said. Remember, the command came to Adam before Eve was even created. Adam could not be deceived. He could only

> **"Firsthand knowledge of God's word eliminates all possibility of deception."**

disobey because he knew the word of God firsthand. The only way a person can be deceived, when it comes to the things of God, is when they are operating only on what they have heard secondhand. We cannot be deceived with first-hand knowledge; we can only disobey as Adam did. That is why it is so vitally important to study the word of God and renew our minds to God's purpose for ourselves. Firsthand knowledge of God's word eliminates all possibility of deception. That is what the Apostle Paul recorded in the New Testament.

> *And Adam was not deceived, but the woman being deceived was in the transgression.*
>
> *1 Timothy 2:14*

Adam could not be deceived because of his knowledge. He had to disobey. Eve was a candidate for deception because of secondhand knowledge and fell for the deception. That is why Jesus had to be born a man and to a woman who was a virgin. A woman had to receive and give birth to the seed of truth (which was lacking in Eve). A man, Jesus (the second Adam), had to be completely obedient (where Adam failed) to the plan of God.

Because of his sin, Adam lost his position of authority and traded the life and nature of God for a carnal lifestyle. Eternal life was exchanged for death, prosperity for poverty, dominion for bondage, health for sickness, etc. Jesus came to redeem us from the curse that came to all mankind because of Adam's disobedience. The curse reversal in our lives begins when we are born again (confessing Jesus as Lord and committing our lives to serving Him). Our spirit man is made alive unto God and we are reconciled unto the Father.

> *Therefore if any man be in Christ, he is a new creature: old things are passed away; behold, all things are become new. And all things are of God, who hath reconciled us to himself by Jesus Christ . . .*
>
> *2 Corinthians 5:17-18a*

I am firmly convinced that the greatest enemy we will ever face is not found in the demonic realm but in the mirror. Our fight will be that of ensuring that the armor of God is firmly in place in our lives. **It is a fight.** If a lifestyle of standing firm upon the word of God was easy, everyone would be doing it. Unfortunately, man as his greatest enemy, finds it easier to explain away the promises of God. The way we will appropriate everything God has given to us is with a true understanding of God's word. This type of understanding does not come because we attend church. This understanding comes because we diligently seek out the truth of God's word for ourselves.

The Westminster Confession includes three items which I find interesting: (1) Nothing contrary to the word of God can be true; (2) Nothing in addition to scripture can be binding; (3) It is the responsibility of every believer to search the scripture for themselves to know what is contained within it.

> **"If a lifestyle of standing firm upon the word of God was easy, everyone would be doing it."**

The way we will successfully accomplish this task is by renewing our minds to the word of God. It is through the knowledge and understanding of the word of God that we will be able to defeat the ultimate enemy; the enemy of carnal thinking which pervades the thoughts of man. We can overcome and rise above the thinking that would keep us in bondage and compromise or destroy our destiny in God.

Keys to Remember

The Ultimate Enemy

❑ God created man to have authority, power and dominion in the planet earth.

❑ The devil doesn't use anything new to deceive.

❑ Satan looks to see if we have any knowledge, then questions our understanding. Second, he will try to get us to question the validity of the word. Last, if we won't deny the word, he will put a deceptive twist upon it so we have the wrong meaning.

❑ The only way a person can be deceived, when it comes to the things of God, is when they are operating only on what they have heard secondhand.

❑ The greatest enemy we will ever face is not found in the demonic realm but in the mirror.

CHAPTER TEN

Renewing the Mind

As I have stated, I believe the ultimate enemy to our Christian walk is not found in the arena of the spirit, but in the mirror. The way we are going to be victorious over this enemy is by exchanging our way of thinking for God's. We call this process renewing the mind. I believe this to be the most important task after a person is born again. I will not go into a long discourse on why we should renew our minds. There are several great books on the subject of renewing the mind and most of us understand the need to do so. What we often lack is the practical how-to's of operating in this process we call renewing the mind!

As a Pastor, I understand the struggles that people go through when they are trying to break free of habits that have been developed over their lifetimes. As a psychologist, I understand the behavioral dynamics that have helped condition the mind to respond under certain situations. Therefore, I will attempt to handle this topic from the standpoint of breaking patterns of failure by operating in true spiritual warfare—the ability to appropriate and enact the word of God in any given situation or circumstance. True warfare is what will be effective on a daily basis, enabling us to stand and reversing prior lifestyles to which we have become accustomed. Such lifestyles have robbed us of the blessings that come because of God's favor.

Before many of us made Jesus Lord, we had established patterns in our lives. These patterns apart from God had a predetermined outcome . . . failure. Momentary glimpses of success often hid the true destination of the paths we had chosen. Most of these patterns were established in selfishness. Our motivation was not to benefit others, but ourselves. As a result, we established our own rules of engagement for the situations with which we were involved—rules whereby we could maintain control. Such patterns led us to wrong conclusions because selfishness contains no wisdom.

At some point in our lives, we recognized the need for God and committed our lives to Him. That was a new beginning. We heard we needed to renew our minds but struggled with our daily priorities. Finding time for God, His word and prayer became secondary. Then the guilt of our inadequacies would settle in along with discouragement and we would quit trying. My goal is to alleviate the discouragement of willpower and find the courage in fighting the good fight of faith. Let me enumerate a few suggestions to help us on this path of renewing the mind that will enhance our ability to stand in true spiritual warfare.

> **"Only through the Lord Jesus Christ and the power of the cross is one able to walk free from the bondage of the past."**

First, one needs to realize their need for God. Don't forget the circumstances that led to your decision to follow Christ. Only through the Lord Jesus Christ and the power of the cross is one able to walk free from the bondage of the past. Jesus must become Lord, not just in name, but in practice. The things of God must become a priority if success is to be achieved.

> **But seek ye first the kingdom of God, and his righteousness;** *and all these things shall be added unto you.*
> Matthew 6:33

How often we seek the success which is only added after we have established God's kingdom as a priority in our lives. Bypassing this priority sets the stage for failure in our lives even before we begin.

Second, change your behavior patterns. This is probably the biggest area that becomes a stumbling block to future success in God. Those who have a problem with drinking refuse to change the places or the people they previously hung out with. Don't fool yourself. *You cannot do what you have always done and expect different results.* Change is a necessity. If you have wrestled with any habit that is contrary to God's life and nature, you must change your environment. Here are a few different translations of our text.

> *Don't become like the people of this world. Instead, change the way you think. Then you will always be able to determine what God really wants—what is good, pleasing, and perfect.*
> Romans 12:2 (GOD'S WORD)

I APPEAL to you therefore, brethren, *and* beg of you in view of [all] the mercies of God, to make a decisive dedication of your bodies—[presenting all your members and faculties]—as a living sacrifice, holy (devoted, consecrated) and well pleasing to God, which is your reasonable (rational, intelligent) service *and* spiritual worship. Do not be conformed to this world—(this age), [fashioned after and adapted to its external, superficial customs], but be transformed (changed) by the [entire] renewal of your mind—[by its new ideals and its new attitude]—so that you may prove [for yourselves] what is the good and acceptable and perfect will of God, *even* the thing which is good and acceptable and perfect [in His sight for you].

Romans 12:1-2 (AMP)

So here's what I want you to do, God helping you: Take your everyday, ordinary life—your sleeping, eating, going-to-work, and walking-around life—and place it before God as an offering. Embracing what God does for you is the best thing you can do for him. Don't become so well-adjusted to your culture that you fit into it without even thinking. Instead, fix your attention on God. You'll be changed from the inside out. Readily recognize what he wants from you, and quickly respond to it. Unlike the culture around you, always dragging you down to its level of immaturity, God brings the best out of you, develops well-formed maturity in you.

Romans 12:1-2 (THE MESSAGE)

How do we change behavior patterns to honor God? Stay out of the bar if you had a drinking problem. Compliment your wife or husband instead of tearing them down. Don't return to the places where you bought your drugs. Avoid the internet sites you frequented if you wrestle with pornography. Quit flirting with that secretary or boss that flatters you. Speak the truth. Whenever you find yourself trying to rationalize or justify any of the actions that are damaging to your walk with God, just admit the error and change. Such rationalization is nothing more than the skin of the truth stuffed with a lie. Make a conscious effort to change your daily habits and routines. Form new habits in your life that will honor God.

Third, become accountable and honest with someone. Be very careful here. I am not suggesting that you simply open up your darkest secrets to anyone. That is a fast way to get burned.

> *Confess your faults one to another, and pray one for another, that ye may be healed. The effectual fervent prayer of a righteous man availeth much.*
>
> *James 5:16*

I believe the key to this verse is not the confession, but to whom you confess. The word says, "The effectual fervent prayer of a **righteous man** . . ." We need to become accountable to those who are in right standing with God and who will protect our mistakes as if they were their own. Someone who will stand with us as we fight the good fight of faith and lift us up before the throne of God in intercession.

Fourth, form new habits and hang out with people who will share your vision of succeeding in God. Don't pay attention to those who try to tell you that your vision is only a "pipe dream" and can never be realized. Avoid those whose only conversation is negative about the church, its leaders, or those in authority. Instead, honor the men and women of God that have been placed in your life to develop you. Establish the attitude of a servant within your heart and let it be reflected toward those who surround you. Dare to be different and stand upon a foundation that is sure. This is the foundation of God's word.

> **Seek ye the LORD** *while he may be found, call ye upon him while he is near: Let the wicked forsake his way, and the unrighteous man his thoughts: and let him* **return unto the LORD, and he will have mercy upon him;** *and to our God, for he will abundantly pardon.* **For my thoughts are not your thoughts, neither are your ways my ways, saith the LORD. For as the heavens are higher than the earth, so are my ways higher than your ways, and my thoughts than your thoughts.** *For as the rain cometh down, and the snow from heaven, and returneth not thither, but watereth the earth, and maketh it bring forth and bud, that it may give seed to the sower, and bread to the eater:* **So shall my word be** *that goeth forth out of my mouth:* **it shall not return unto me void, but it shall accomplish that which I please, and it shall prosper in the thing whereto I sent it.**
>
> *Isaiah 55:6-11*

Seek God and adopt His way of thinking. His ways are so much better than ours. His ways work. They *always* work! This is the basic principle of renewing the mind. Exchange your life for His by adopting His way of thinking over yours. Sounds simple, doesn't it? So where is the problem in our daily walks?

> *Many are the plans in a man's heart, but it is the LORD's purpose that prevails.*
>
> *Proverbs 19:21 (NIV)*

There are several things that I have tried on my own and failed. Isaiah said God's word never fails. I want the 100% success rate that God has. It is God's purpose that always prevails. True humility is not pretending to be a worm, but recognizing and accepting God's ways are far greater, and then submitting to them. I want to be quick to hear God's voice and quick to respond. I do not want my environment to dictate my actions. I want to rise above the standards of society by acknowledging that God is greater than I am. I will submit myself to the transforming power of God's unchanging word.

Nobody forced me to make Jesus Lord. Nobody is twisting my arm to serve Him. I became a believer in Jesus because I made a personal choice. I am not the type of person who just wanted some shadow of religiosity in my life.

> **"True humility is . . .**
> **accepting God's ways . . .**
> **and then submitting to them."**

When I made up my mind to serve Jesus, it was an all-out commitment: None of this halfhearted, watered down stuff for me. I want all that God has for me and it only stands to reason that He would want all that I am for Him. This must be a two-way relationship. Therefore, I will take my everyday ordinary life—all that I am and all that I will do—and commit it to Him. This means that I must be willing to give up my life for His. Not a bad exchange if you ask me.

If we will have the courage to change our daily habits and environment for the things of the kingdom of God, I am convinced we will succeed. As God instructed Joshua,

This book of the law shall not depart out of thy mouth; but thou shalt **meditate therein day and night, that thou mayest observe to do** *according to all that is written therein:* **for then thou shalt make thy way prosperous, and then thou shalt have good success.**

Joshua 1:8

This is the process of renewing our minds that will enhance our daily lives in the Lord Jesus—not just hearing or reading God's word, but being willing to *"appropriate and enact"* God's word. Many people simply hear the word of God but never "do" the word of God. Through a renewed mind we can, "fight the good fight of faith," and understand the mind-set of the Apostle Paul when he instructed the church at Ephesus to stand.

Put on the whole armour of God, that ye may be able to stand *against the wiles of the devil. For we wrestle not against flesh and blood, but against principalities, against powers, against the rulers of the darkness of this world, against spiritual wickedness in high places.* **Wherefore take unto you the whole armour of God, that ye may be able to withstand in the evil day, and having done all, to stand. Stand . . .**

Ephesians 6:11-14a

Renewing the mind is the key to our success. True spiritual warfare is not the ability to control demons, but to control ourselves: Allowing our thoughts to become God's thoughts and thereby elevating ourselves to His level by the power of the Holy Spirit.

Keys to Remember

Renewing the Mind

❏ The way we are going to be victorious over this enemy is by exchanging our way of thinking for God's. We call this process renewing the mind.

❏ Change your behavior patterns. *You cannot do what you have always done and expect different results.*

❏ Become accountable and honest with someone.

❏ Form new habits and hang out with people who will share your vision of succeeding in God.

❏ Renewing the mind is the key to our success.

❏ True spiritual warfare is not the ability to control demons, but to control ourselves.

CHAPTER ELEVEN

Finally

Finally, my brethren, be strong in the Lord,
and in the power of his might.
Ephesians 6:10

The Apostle Paul makes it clear that we are to be strong in the Lord and the power of His might. If we will take the time to be strong in the Lord by renewing our minds to the word of God, devils will never be our problem. Those who are going to be involved in true spiritual warfare—the ability to appropriate and enact the word of God in any given situation or circumstance—and fight the good fight of faith are those who daily exercise the word of God in their lives. We must be able to recognize God's word as truth and allow that truth to cause us to be able to overcome the facts presented in our lives.

There is much we can learn from the Apostle Paul's letter to the church at Ephesus. I believe we can find a pattern for true spiritual warfare within its pages. I too pray that the eyes of our understanding would be opened so we can truly see the wonderful life that has been given to us by Jesus' sacrifice on the cross. Once we realize who we are in Christ and then begin to fulfill our responsibilities within the local church as a part of the body, devils will no longer be our focus or problem.

Are devils real? Absolutely! But when the word of God has become our armor, the devil is no match for us. We are the children of God with all authority and power and there is no demonic entity that can stand against us. We arc the ones who will be standing and the gates of hell cannot prevail.

> *When Jesus came into the coasts of Caesarea Philippi, he asked his disciples, saying, Whom do men say that I the Son of man am? And they said, Some say that thou art John the Baptist: some, Elias; and others, Jeremias, or one of the prophets. He saith unto them,* **But whom say ye that I am?** *And Simon Peter answered and said,* **Thou art the Christ, the Son of the living God.** *And Jesus answered and said unto him, Blessed art thou, Simon Barjona: for flesh and blood hath not revealed it unto thee, but my Father which is in heaven. And I say also unto thee, That thou art Peter, and* **upon this rock I will build my church; and the gates of hell shall not prevail against it.**
> *Matthew 16:13-18*

The foundational key to spiritual warfare is not found in our knowledge of who the devil is, but in our knowledge of who Jesus is. It is upon this rock of revelation that the church was built and it will be upon this rock that it is maintained. Jesus must be the focus of our lives and confession.

True spiritual warfare is the ability to appropriate and enact the word of God in any given situation and circumstance. If a devil stands between us and our destiny, cast him out, but do not let demons become your focus. Let us appropriate what God has provided and stand firm in the word of God.

Keys to Remember

Finally

❑ Take the time to be strong in the Lord by renewing our minds and devils will never be our problem.

❑ We must be able to recognize God's word as truth and allow that truth to cause us to be able to overcome the facts presented in our lives.

❑ We are the children of God with all authority and power and there is no demonic entity that can stand against us.

❑ True spiritual warfare is the ability to appropriate and enact the word of God in any given situation and circumstance.

Author Contact

For more information about books, tapes, or CD's, please write:

Dr. Lonny Bingle
Spokane Faith Center
3330 W Central
Spokane, WA 99205
USA
(509) 327-9673

Or contact us at:

www.spokanefaithcenter.org